**Herkimer County
Community College Library
Herkimer, New York
13350**

1. Books may be kept for three weeks and may be renewed once, except when otherwise noted.

2. Reference books, such as dictionaries and encyclopedias are to be used only in the Library.

3. A fine is charged for each day a book is not returned according to the above rule.

4. All injuries to books beyond reasonable wear and all losses shall be made good to the satisfaction of the Librarian.

5. Each borrower is held responsible for all books drawn on his card and for all fines accruing on the same.

LAW ENFORCEMENT CAREER GUIDE
NEW YORK

LEARNINGEXPRESS

NEW YORK

Library of Congress Cataloging-in-Publication Data

Law enforcement career guide : New York.
    p.   cm. — (The LearningExpress law enforcement library)
  Includes index.
  ISBN 1-57685-007-2
  1. Law enforcement—New York (State)—Examinations, questions,
etc. 2. Law enforcement—Vocational guidance—New York (State)
3. Employment tests—New York (State) I. LearningExpress
(Organization) II. Series.
  HV8145.N7L39 1996
  363.2′023′747—dc20

96-4719
CIP

Printed in the United States of America
9 8 7 6 5 4 3 2 1
First Edition

Regarding the Information in this Book
We attempt to verify the information presented in our books prior to publication. It is always a good idea, however, to double-check such important information as minimum requirements, application and testing procedures, and deadlines with your local law enforcement agency, as such information can change from time to time.

For Further Information
For information on LearningExpress, other LearningExpress products, or bulk sales, please call or write to us at:
    LearningExpress™
    900 Broadway
    Suite 604
    New York, NY 10003
    212-995-2566

LearningExpress is an affiliated company of Random House, Inc.

271-PD-8-(10.6)

ISBN 1-57685-007-2

7 85555 85007 1

CONTENTS

LIST OF CONTRIBUTORS

The following individuals contributed to the content of this book.

Susan Camardo is a business and careers writer and communications consultant based in New York City.

Jan Gallagher, Ph.D., is a test-development specialist, editor, and teacher living in Jersey City, New Jersey.

Mary Hesalroad, a former police officer for the Austin, Texas, Police Department, consults with police departments on recruiting efforts and is a freelance writer now living in Alameda, California.

Karen Petty is a New York City-based writer specializing in career development issues.

Judith Schlesinger, Ph.D., is a writer and psychologist whose background includes years of working with police officers in psychiatric crisis interventions.

The following LearningExpress staff members also contributed to the writing and researching of this book: **Jean Eckhoff, Edward Grossman,** and **Pamela Harrell.**

C·H·A·P·T·E·R

LAW ENFORCEMENT CAREERS IN NEW YORK

1

CHAPTER SUMMARY

This chapter provides a useful introduction to the many helpful resources you'll find in this book. It features recruiting contacts at the state police and major police and sheriff's departments in New York plus a listing of state correctional facilities. Also included is a sample job application to show you what kind of information law enforcement agencies want to know about you right off the bat.

You must be the type of person who wants to make a smart career choice. That's clear because you decided to get the right kind of information to help you make that choice. You want to know what you're getting into and what it will take to get there. In other words, you're thinking ahead—which happens to be especially important for the careers described in this book.

Since you encounter law enforcement professionals all the time—in your community and in the movies and on television, among other places—you already have some general knowledge of this field. But if you're going to enter the field yourself, you need specifics. From this book you'll find out:

- what kind of candidates law enforcement agencies are looking for
- how the application process works

- the requirements you'll have to meet before you can apply
- the testing procedures you'll go through to be selected
- the training and education you'll need to succeed

Along with learning about the selection process, you'll come across a number of valuable tips about how to make yourself an attractive candidate and increase your chances of getting hired.

THE REAL DEAL

Before you travel down this road, however, you'll want to know what a "day in the life" of a law enforcement officer is really like—the duties you'll have, the working environment, the job prospects and so forth. The next three chapters ahead give you that detailed view for three major career areas: municipal police, state police and corrections officers. A later chapter takes a broader look at the many career paths open to you in this field, including law enforcement positions with the federal government and related occupations in the private sector.

Another thing you'll be considering, of course, is whether these careers suit your personality and temperament. Several key traits that law enforcement officers need to have are covered throughout this book. To personalize things, you can take the "Police Officer Suitability Test." This self-quiz helps you find out whether you have the qualities that tend to make for success as a police officer; many of these apply to any law enforcement position.

Across New York, a wide variety of opportunities are available in law enforcement. You can look into positions with municipal, county or state government agencies. Other sources are regional offices or institutions run by the federal government. This book will help you explore your options.

At the end of this chapter are lists of recruiting contacts for police departments in major cities in New York plus sheriff's departments and the state police. We've also included a list of state correctional facilities. Finally, you'll find a sample application form, which will tell you the sort of information a hiring agency or institution will want to know about you when you first apply. In addition, the chapter on "Law Enforcement Education and Training" includes a list of colleges that offer criminal justice, law enforcement and corrections programs in New York.

WHY BMP IS IMPORTANT

To become a law enforcement officer in New York, you need to know about an organization called the Bureau for Municipal Police (BMP). This agency approves minimum standards for both hiring and training peace officers, which includes municipal police, sheriffs, corrections officers, marshals and other law enforcement professionals.

When officers are selected by law enforcement agencies in New York, they are required to complete a course of training called the Basic Course or Academy. After you pass this training and have submitted proof to the BMP that you have met all the necessary requirements, you receive a Basic Certificate and are registered with the BMP as a full-duty officer.

In addition, other certified training programs are available through the BMP. Throughout your career, you may earn certificates in such areas as breath testing or DARE (Drug Abuse Resistance Education) training. Extra pay and promotions are typical ways that departments recognize officers who earn these professional certificates.

THE REWARDS OF A LAW ENFORCEMENT CAREER

The fact is, every law enforcement career involves public service, hard work and a certain amount of personal risk. That's the case whether you're on the streets enforcing the law or guarding those who have been locked up for breaking the law. Each career also offers a variety of personal rewards beyond the paycheck and benefits.

If you like what you learn about this field, those rewards could be yours. You're taking the first step by arming yourself with information. To keep moving forward, you'll need to set your target, plan your course of action and prepare yourself to pass through the selection process with flying colors. This book will help in those first important steps.

RECRUITING CONTACTS FOR THE TOP 10 POLICE DEPARTMENTS IN NEW YORK

Albany Police Department
Albany Municipal Civil Service Commission
City Hall, Room 256M
Albany, NY 12207
518-434-5052

Binghamton Police Department
City of Binghamton Personnel Department
City Hall, Governor Plaza, Fifth Floor
Binghamton, NY 13901
607-772-7008

Buffalo Police Department
Erie County Department of Personnel
Exam Division
95 Franklin Street
Buffalo, NY 14202
716-858-8484

Nassau County Police Department
1490 Franklin Avenue
Mineola, NY 11501
800-RECRUIT
(800-732-7848)

New York City Police Department
Recruitment Section
280 Broadway, Room 100
New York, NY 1007-1809
212-RECRUIT
(212-732-7848)

Rochester Police Department
City of Rochester Personnel Department
Civic Center Plaza
150 South Plymouth Avenue
Rochester, NY 14614
716-428-6716

Suffolk County Police Department
Recruitment Unit
30 Yaphank Avenue
Yaphank, NY 11980
800-727-3926
516-852-6511

Syracuse Police Department
511 South State Street
Syracuse, NY 13202
315-442-5290

Yonkers Police Department
Recruitment Unit
36 Radford Street
Yonkers, NY 10705
914-377-7375

Westchester County Police
Westchester County Department of Personnel
148 Martine Avenue
White Plains, NY 10601
914-285-2100

RECRUITING CONTACTS FOR THE TOP 10 SHERIFF'S DEPARTMENTS IN NEW YORK

Albany County Sheriff
Albany County Courthouse
Albany, NY 12207
518-487-5400

Broome County Sheriff
Personnel
PO Box 1766
Binghamton, NY 13902
607-778-2185

Erie County Sheriff
Personnel
Rath Building, Room 604
95 Franklin Street
Buffalo, NY 14202
716-858-8484

Monroe County Sheriff
Training Unit
130 South Plymouth Avenue
Rochester, NY 14614
716-428-5432

New York City Sheriff
Department of Personnel
2 Washington Street
New York, NY 10004
212-487-6500

Oneida County Sheriff
Department of Personnel
Onieda County Office Building
800 Park Avenue
Utica, NY 13501
315-798-5725

Onondaga County Sheriff
Justice Center
555 South State Street
Syracuse, NY
315-425-3025

Orange County Sheriff
Orange County Personnel
255 Main Street
Goshen, NY 10924
914-294-5151

Rockland County Sheriff
Rockland County Personnel Office
18 New Hempstead Road
New City, NY 10956
914-638-5200

Schenectady County Sheriff
Civil Service Office
620 State Street
Schenectady, NY 12305
518-388-4270

RECRUITING CONTACT FOR THE NEW YORK STATE POLICE

New York State Police Personnel Office
State Campus, Building 22
Albany, NY 12226
518-457-2758

NEW YORK STATE CORRECTIONAL FACILITIES

New York State Department of Civil Service
Building 1, State Campus
Albany, NY 12239
General information 518-474-2121
Corrections personnel 518-457-7329

The state-run Department of Corrections will place you at one of the following institutions after you successfully complete a selection process and training program:

Adirondack Correctional Facility (CF)
PO Box 110
Ray Brook, NY 12977-0110

Albion CF
3595 State School Road
Albion, NY 14411

Altona CF
Devil Den Road, Box 125
Altona, NY 12910

Arthur Kill CF
2911 Arthur Kill Road
Staten Island, NY 10301

Attica CF
PO Box 149
Attica, NY 14011-0149

Auburn CF
135 State Street
Auburn, NY 13021

Bare Hill CF
Caller Box #20, Cady Road
Malone, NY 12953

Bayview CF
550 West 20th Street
New York, NY 10011-2878

Beacon CF
PO Box 780
Beacon, NY 12508-0780

Bedford Hills CF
247 Harris Road
Bedford Hills, NY 10507-2499

Buffalo CF
P.O. Box 300
Alden, NY 14004

**Butler Alcohol and Substance Abuse
Correctional Treatment Facility (ASACTC)**
Westbury Cut-off Road
PO Box 400
Red Creek, NY 13143

Butler CF
PO Box 388, Route 370
Red Creek, NY 13143

Camp Gabriels
PO Box 100
Gabriels, NY 12939-0100

Camp Georgetown
RD #1, Box 48
Georgetown, NY 13072-9307

Camp Pharsalia
South Plymouth, NY 13844-9729

Cape Vincent CF
Route 12E, Box 599
Cape Vincent, NY 13618

Cayuga CF
PO Box 1150
Moravia, NY 13118

Chateaugay ASACTC
PO Box 320, Route 11
Chateaugay, NY 12920

Clinton CF
PO Box 2000
Dannemora, NY 12929

Collins CF
Helmuth, NY 14078-0200

Coxsackie CF
PO Box 200
West Coxsackie, NY 12051-0200

Downstate CF
PO Box 445
Fishkill, NY 12524-0445

Eastern New York CF
PO Box 338
Napanoch, NY 12458-0338

Edgecombe CF
611 Edgecombe Avenue
New York, NY 10032-4398

Elmira CF
PO Box 500
Elmira, NY 14902-0500

Fishkill CF
PO Box 307
Beacon, NY 12508

Franklin CF
PO Box 10
Malone, NY 12953

Fulton CF
1511 Fulton Avenue
Bronx, NY 10457-8398

Gouverneur CF
PO Box 370
Scotch Settlement Road
Gouverneur, NY 13642-0370

Great Meadow CF
PO Box 51
Comstock, NY 12821

Green Haven CF
Stormville, NY 12582

Greene CF
PO Box 8
Coxsackie, NY 12051-0008

Groveland CF
Route 36, Sonyea Road
Sonyea, NY 14556-0001

Hale Creek ASACTC
279 Maloney Road
Johnstown, NY 12095

Hudson CF
PO Box 576
Hudson, NY 12534-0576

Lakeview Shock Incarceration CF
PO Box T
Brocton, NY 14716

Lincoln CF
31-33 West 110th Street
New York, NY 10026-4398

Livingston CF
PO Box 49
Sonyea, NY 14556

Lyon Mountain CF
PO Box 276
Lyon Mountain, NY 12952-0276

Marcy CF
PO Box 500
Marcy, NY 13403

Mid-Orange CF
900 Kings Highway
Warwick, NY 10990-0900

Mid-State CF
PO Box 216
Marcy, NY 13403-0216

Mohawk CF
PO Box 8450
6100 School Road
Rome, NY 13440

Monterey Shock Incarceration CF
RD #1
2150 Evergreen Hill Road
Beaver Dams, NY 14812-9718

Moriah Shock Incarceration CF
PO Box 99
Mineville, NY 12956-0999

Mt. McGregor CF
PO Box 2071
Wilton, NY 12866-0996

Ogdensburg CF
One Correction Way
Ogdensburg, NY 13669-2288

Oneida CF
6100 School Road
Rome, NY 13440

Orleans CF
35-31 Gaines Basin Road
Albion, NY 14411

Otisville CF
PO Box 8
Otisville, NY 10963-0008

Parkside CF
10 Mt. Morris Park West
New York, NY 10027-6395

Queensboro CF
47-04 Van Dam Street
Long Island City, NY 11101-3081

Riverview CF
PO Box 158
Ogdensburg, NY 12669

Rochester Correctional Facility
470 Ford Street
Rochester, NY 14608-2499

Shawangunk CF
PO Box 750
Wallkill, NY 12589-0750

Sing Sing Correctional Facility
354 Hunter Street
Ossining, NY 10562-5442

Southport CF
PO Box 2000
Pine City, NY 14871

Sullivan CF
Box AG
Fallsburg, NY 12733-0116

Summit Shock Incarceration CF
RFD
Summit, NY 12175

Taconic CF
250 Harris Road
Bedford Hills, NY 10507-2498

Ulster CF
Berme Road
PO Box 800
Napanoch, NY 12458

Wallkill CF
Box G
Wallkill, NY 12589-0286

Washington CF
PO Box 180
Comstock, NY 12821-0180

Watertown CF
Dry Hill
Watertown, NY 13601-0168

Wende CF
PO Box 1187
Alden, NY 14004-1187

Woodbourne CF
Riverside Drive
Woodbourne, NY 12788

Wyoming CF
PO Box 501
Attica, NY 14011

INSTRUCTIONS AND BIO-DATA RESEARCH QUESTIONNAIRE

Complete the application on pages 1 and 2, following the directions below. Since the application will be "read" by machine, you must take great care in completing it. Use a No. 2 pencil only. Do **not** use a pen. Erase errors completely. Do not make stray marks on the application. Fill in the circles with heavy black marks.

1. EXAMINATION TITLE: Fill in the circle preceding the examination for which you are applying. **You may only select one examination per application.** Refer to the official examination announcement for the minimum qualifications and other information regarding the examination for which you are applying. There are minimum age requirements for Police Officer, Correction Officer I and Deputy Sheriff I/Park Ranger I.

2. NAME: Start at the left margin of each section. Print as much of your name as possible in the boxes provided, one letter in each box. Omit spaces, hyphens, and apostrophes. Do not go beyond the boxes provided, even if you cannot fit all the information in those boxes. If there are more boxes than needed, leave them blank. The MI box is for your middle initial. Then fill in the circle below each box that has the same letter as the box.

3. SOCIAL SECURITY NUMBER: Write your social security number in the boxes provided. Then fill in the appropriate circle below each box number. **Take special care to make sure this number is entered accurately!**

4. DATE OF BIRTH: Fill in the circle for the month in which you were born. Then write the day and last two digits of the year that you were born in the boxes provided, and fill in the appropriate circles. (The date of birth is not required for Probation Officer Trainee applicants.)

Note: The first nine days of each month must be entered as 01, 02, 03, etc.

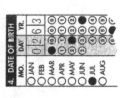

5. DAYTIME TELEPHONE NUMBER: Write your daytime telephone number including area code in the boxes provided. Then fill in the appropriate circles.

6. QUESTIONS A–D: Answer each of these questions. Fill in the appropriate circle after each question and provide any required information in the comments section. A yes answer is not an automatic bar to employment. Each case is considered and evaluated on its individual merits. Background investigations will be conducted on all candidates considered for employment. A false statement may result in your disqualification.

7. SATURDAY SABBATH OBSERVER: If you are a Saturday sabbath observer who, for religious reasons only, requests permission to take this examination after sundown on Saturday, fill in the yes circle. If you mark yes, you will be asked to provide verification.

8. SPECIAL ACCOMMODATIONS: If you need special accommodations to participate in this examination fill in the yes circle and describe the type of assistance you request in the comments section.

9. PROBATION OFFICER TRAINEE APPLICANTS ONLY: The minimum qualifications for Probation Officer Trainee and Probation Officer Trainee (Spanish Speaking) require a Bachelor's Degree including at least thirty semester credit hours in the social or behavioral sciences. Indicate if you meet these minimum qualifications. You must submit a copy of your college transcript with your application.

10. VETERANS' CREDITS: Veterans' credits are granted on the following basis:

NON-DISABLED VETERANS: 5 points for Open-Competitive Exams
DISABLED VETERANS: 10 points for Open-Competitive Exams

These additional credits, which are combined with the final score obtained in the examination, may be granted only to PASSING CANDIDATES at the time of establishment of the eligible list.

Non-Disabled Veterans
In order to be eligible for additional credits as a non-disabled veteran, you must:
1. Have served on full-time ACTIVE DUTY, other than active duty for training purposes, with the Armed Forces of the United States during any of the following periods:

VIETNAM	- December 22, 1961 through and including May 7, 1975
LEBANON*	- June 1, 1983 through and including December 1, 1987
GRENADA*	- October 23, 1983 through and including November 21, 1983
PANAMA*	- December 20, 1989 through and including January 31, 1990
PERSIAN GULF	- August 2, 1990 - to the end of the hostilities as yet undefined

*To receive veterans' credits for service in these campaigns, an applicant must also have been the recipient of one of the following:

Armed Forces Expeditionary Medal
Navy Expeditionary Medal
Marine Corps Expeditionary Medal

2. Have been honorably discharged or released under honorable conditions from such service.

3. Submit a photocopy of separation papers (ie. FORM DD-214 (member 4 copy) or equivalent) from the Armed Forces of the United States before this eligible list is established.

4. Complete question number 10 on the application.

Disabled Veterans

In order to be eligible for additional credits as a disabled veteran, in addition to meeting the requirements of items 1, 2, 3 & 4 listed above, you must also complete Form VC-3 (Authorization For Disability Record) in duplicate and forward BOTH copies immediately to the Regional Office of the United States Veterans Administration where your application for disability pension is on file. The Veterans Administration will retain a copy for its files, and will return a copy to this Department for processing. Disabled veterans must have a war-incurred disability of at least ten percent (10%) certified by the Veterans Administration at the time of application for additional credits.

Civil Service Law limits the use of veterans' credits to one permanent competitive class appointment within New York State. If you do not forward the proper documentation as outlined above, you will not be granted veterans' credits. Once the eligible list is established, veterans' credits cannot be granted.

11. MAILING ADDRESS: Start at the left margin. Enter as much of your address as possible in the boxes provided. Leave spaces as required in your house number and street name. If you have an apartment number, enter the number at the end of the line for street address. Use a hyphen where required. Abbreviate the street address if necessary (see abbreviations below). Then fill in the appropriate circles. You must notify the Suffolk County Department of Civil Service in writing if your address changes. If your address has changed since you last filed an application, fill in the address change circle.

Example: If you live at 24–13 East 123rd Street, Apartment 44G, you should enter your address as follows:

11. MAILING ADDRESS: Street (leave spaces as required)

2	4	-	1	3		E		1	2	3	R	D		S	T		4	4	G

APPROVED U.S. POSTAL SERVICE ABBREVIATIONS
For Street Addresses

Apartment	APT	Highway	HWY	Road	RD
Avenue	AVE	Lake	LK	Route	RT
Boulevard	BLVD	Lane	LA	South	S
Box	BX	Mount	MT	Street	ST
Broadway	BDWY	Mountain	MT	Terrace	TR
Court	CT	North	N	Trail	TRL
Drive	DR	Park	PK	Trailer	TRLR
East	E	Parkway	PKWY	Turnpike	TPKE
Fort	FT	Pike	PI	Way	WY
Garden	GDN	Place	PL	West	W
Headquarters	HQ	Point	PT		
Heights	HTS	Port	PT		

12. CITY/POST OFFICE and STATE: Enter the name of your City/Post Office and the two-letter abbreviation for your state. Then fill in the appropriate circles.

13. ZIP CODE: Start at the left margin and enter your ZIP code in the spaces provided. The last +4 numbers are optional. Then fill in the appropriate circles.

14. LEGAL RESIDENCE CODES: Fill in codes from the following list:

COUNTY	CODE
Suffolk County	1
Other	0

TOWNS	CODE
Babylon	01
Brookhaven	02
East Hampton	03
Huntington	04
Islip	05
Riverhead	06
Shelter Island	07
Smithtown	08
Southampton	09
Southold	10
Other	00

INCORPORATED VILLAGES			
Amityville	01	Nissequogue	15
Asharoken	02	North Haven	16
Babylon	03	Northport	17
Belle Terre	04	Ocean Beach	18
Bellport	05	Old Field	19
Brightwaters	06	Patchogue	20
Dering Harbor	07	Poquott	21
East Hampton	08	Port Jefferson	22
Greenport	09	Quogue	23
Head-of-the-Harbor	10	Sag Harbor	24
Huntington Bay	11	Saltaire	25
Islandia	30	Shoreham	26
Lake Grove	12	Southampton	27
Lindenhurst	13	Village of the Branch	28
Lloyd Harbor	14	Westhampton Beach	29
		Other	00

15. LEGAL ADDRESS: Enter the address of your legal residence if it is different from your mailing address.

16. DECLARATION: Sign and date the declaration.
If you attach any additional sheets, print your name and social security number on them.
Return the completed application to: Suffolk County Department of Civil Service
220 Rabro Drive P.O. Box 6100
Hauppauge, NY 11788-0099

BIO-DATA RESEARCH QUESTIONNAIRE

Completion of this questionnaire is voluntary. This information will be used in research and in connection with affirmative action efforts.

Fill in the appropriate circle   **SEX**   ○ Female   ○ Male

FILL IN THE ONE CIRCLE THAT DESCRIBES YOUR ETHNIC ORIGIN

○ **American Indian or Alaskan Native**—A person who has origins in any of the original peoples of North America and who maintains tribal affiliation or community recognition.

○ **Hispanic**—A person of Puerto Rican, Mexican, Cuban, Central or South American or other Spanish culture or origin, regardless of race.

○ **Asian or Pacific Islander**—A person who has origins in any of the original peoples of the Far East, Southeast Asia, the Indian subcontinent, or the Pacific Islands. This area includes, for example, China, Japan, Korea, the Philippine Islands and Samoa.

○ **White** (not of Hispanic origin)—A person who has origins in any of the original peoples of Europe, North Africa or the Middle East.

○ **Black** (not of Hispanic origin)—A person who has origins in any of the black racial groups of Africa.

○ **Other**

SUFFOLK COUNTY APPLICATION FOR LAW ENFORCEMENT CS-205LE

FOR OFFICE USE ONLY

SUFFOLK COUNTY DEPARTMENT OF CIVIL SERVICE
220 RABRO DRIVE P.O. BOX 6100
HAUPPAUGE, NEW YORK 11788-0099

Suffolk County does not discriminate against any applicant because of race, creed, color, national origin, handicap, sex, age, marital status or sexual preference.

THE APPLICATION PROCESSING FEE IS $50.00. Your application MUST be accompanied by a $50 NON-REFUNDABLE NON-TRANSFERABLE application processing fee. DO NOT SEND CASH. Make your check or money order payable to the Suffolk County Department of Civil Service. Please indicate the examination title and your social security number on the face of your check or money order.

Read the directions on pages 3 and 4 as you complete the application.

Mark Reflex® by NCS EM-160064:654321   A1101   Printed in U.S.A.

1. EXAMINATION TITLE: Fill in the circle preceding the examination for which you are applying. You may only select one examination per application.

- ○ Correction Officer I
- ○ Deputy Sheriff I/Park Ranger I
- ○ Police Officer
- ○ Probation Officer Trainee
- ○ Probation Officer Trainee (Spanish Speaking)

2. LAST NAME (Print)

FIRST NAME

MI

3. SOCIAL SECURITY NUMBER

4. DATE OF BIRTH

MO. / DAY / YR.

JAN, FEB, MAR, APR, MAY, JUN, JUL, AUG, SEP, OCT, NOV, DEC

5. DAYTIME TELEPHONE NUMBER

AREA CODE

APPLICATION FOR LAW ENFORCEMENT

11. MAILING ADDRESS: Street (leave spaces as required)

12. CITY/POST OFFICE

STATE

13. ZIP CODE + 4

14. LEGAL RESIDENCE
COUNTY | TOWN | VILLAGE

ADDRESS CHANGE

6. Fill in the appropriate circle

	Yes	No
A. Have you ever been convicted of a crime (felony or misdemeanor)?	Y	N
B. Were you ever dismissed or discharged from any employment for reasons other than lack of work or funds?	Y	N
C. Did you ever resign from any employment rather than face dismissal?	Y	N
D. Did you ever receive a discharge from the Armed Forces of the United States which was other than honorable or which was issued under other than honorable circumstances?	Y	N

If you answered YES to any question A–D you MUST give specifics in the comments section below.

7. Are you a Saturday sabbath observer who, for religious reasons only, requests permission to take this examination after sundown on Saturday?

○ Yes ○ No

8. Do you need special accommodations to participate in this examination?

○ Yes ○ No

9. Probation Officer Trainee and Probation Officer Trainee (Spanish Speaking) applicants only. Do you have a Bachelor's Degree including at least thirty semester credit hours in the social or behavioral sciences?

○ Yes ○ No

You must submit a copy of your college transcript with this application.

10. VETERANS' CREDITS:

A. Do you wish to claim veterans' credits?

○ Yes, as a non-disabled veteran
○ Yes, as a disabled veteran
○ No

If you answered yes, complete B and submit separation papers (Form DD-214) before the eligible list is established

B. If you have ever been employed by a governmental agency in New York State complete the following:

Government Name _____

Length of Employment From _____ To _____
(Attach additional sheets if necessary)

COMMENTS _____

15. If your address has changed since you last filed an application, fill in the circle. ○

LEGAL ADDRESS (If different from mailing address)

CITY _____ STATE _____ ZIP CODE _____

16. DECLARATION: I declare, subject to the penalties of perjury, that the statements made in this application (including statements made in any accompanying papers) have been examined by me and to the best of my knowledge and belief are true and correct. I further request and authorize any former or present employer, military records center, police, parole, and probation agencies, and former school to provide to the Suffolk County, Department of Civil Service any and all information including, but not limited to information as to my character, habits, work ability, and/or education. In consideration of compliance with this request, I hereby release and discharge said institutions from any claims, liabilities, or damages.

C·H·A·P·T·E·R

LIFE BEHIND THE BADGE: THE WORK OF A POLICE OFFICER

CHAPTER SUMMARY

Congratulations! You've decided to find out about police work as a possible career choice for yourself. This first chapter will tell you what police work involves, from the variety of tasks you can expect to be doing to the skills and traits a police officer needs. You'll also find out about the latest trends in police departments and long-term career opportunities.

o you're in great shape. You can do multiple sit-ups with ease. You can run up and down stairs time and again and barely become winded. A wall climb or an obstacle course? No problem. Your vision is perfect, your heart sound, and you can hear a pin drop a block away. You'd pass any medical exam with flying colors.

If you want to join the police force, all that counts. Police work requires stamina, agility and strength. But having a healthy body or 20/20 eyesight is only one measure of whether or not you're suited for the job.

It takes a lot to be a good police officer. To give you some idea, you'll need to be able to:

- Read human behavior
- Cope with high levels of stress
- Communicate with all types of people

- Learn the law
- Have an eye for detail and a knack for paperwork
- Serve as a good leader, role model, negotiator and problem-solver
- Help people in a caring manner while keeping some emotional distance and
- Be ready to put your life on the line at any time

If it sounds like you need the qualities of a psychologist, air traffic controller, teacher, lawyer, accountant, politician, doctor and firefighter all rolled up into one—well, yes, that's just about the size of it. What's more, you'll go through a rigorous and often lengthy process just to get accepted as a police recruit. That tests your level of motivation right off the bat. You have to really want this job to persevere and succeed at each part of the application process.

HAVE YOU GOT WHAT IT TAKES?

Police departments use the application process to evaluate certain qualities that can make or break your competence as an officer. It's true that there's no exact science to measure such key traits as honesty and integrity. Yet the series of tests that police candidates are put through—written, oral and physical exams—is designed by experts to offer departments a reliable indication of an applicant's general character and abilities.

For example, police departments are looking for candidates with emotional stability. They're looking for a sense of responsibility and a clear respect for authority. At the same time, they want to know that you are able to make decisions independently and exercise good judgment. An important point here is that departments want recruits who care about helping people *from all walks of life*—of every race, religion, sex, sexual preference, age, or socioeconomic class. This goes for the people you work with as well as the public you serve. Police officers are obliged to treat all people equally and equitably under the law. That same attitude and behavior are what police candidates need to express.

SKILLS YOU'LL NEED

Qualifications described above have to do with a person's temperament, personality and belief system. But police departments look for certain basic skills as well.

For example, you can expect your communication skills to be tested. You don't have to be the world's greatest public speaker or write like an English professor. However, police work does involve a constant processing of information, both spoken and written. As an officer, you'll need to prepare daily activity reports. You'll be interviewing witnesses and negotiating with possible informants. You'll have to clearly understand orders and department policies handed down by superior officers. You'll be settling disputes and calming down people in crisis situations. These and many other tasks call for an ability to express yourself effectively and to interact well with other people. That means the *way* you interact matters, too—for instance, being tactful, cooperative and not condescending, even if you happen to be dealing with people who are disrespectful, hostile or just plain aggravating. It'll be up to you to keep your cool.

Some skills that are desirable in a police officer can't necessarily be "taught," although they can be developed or improved through practice and focus. Having a good memory, good powers of observation, and reliable instincts about people and situations are examples. Part of the job, after all, is being able to do such things as recall what a fleeing suspect was wearing, scope out evidence at a crime scene, and pick up on suspicious behavior. And part of the tests you'll take to become an officer will be aimed at measuring these kinds of abilities.

SKILLS YOU'LL LEARN

Many skills will be taught to police officer candidates once they've made it through the application process and been accepted as a recruit. For instance, you don't need to know how to use firearms or administer first aid to pass the entrance exams. These are skills you'll learn as part of your professional training. You'll also be taught self-defense techniques, patrol and traffic control procedures, the use of police equipment and vehicles, emergency measures, and a variety of other strategies and tactics. On small or rural forces, new recruits often get the bulk of their professional training on the job, working closely with an experienced officer. Larger departments typically require a period of formal training, often weeks or months in a police academy or other academic setting. Classroom instruction is then followed by a period of on-the-job or field training.

You also won't need to have specific knowledge about laws or the legal system before you take the police entrance exams. Police departments include this kind of instruction in their training programs for new recruits. That's when they'll make sure that you are up to speed on state and local laws, constitutional rights, civil rights and other areas relevant to law enforcement.

As you can see, police officers are highly trained professionals. And with good reason. As an officer, you'll be trusted with no less of a mission than ensuring the safety and well being of your community. Because of that trust, you will face high expectations in performing your job and be held to the highest standards of behavior. An officer's work is demanding, difficult and always potentially dangerous. All in all,

there's a lot more to policing than enforcing the law. There's also a lot less gritty glamour and excitement than most TV shows and movies portray. Still, it's a job that carries many rewards for the right kind of person. Policing offers you a chance to do important and interesting work—and work that you can be proud of.

THE POLICE OFFICER: ON THE JOB

If you like having a variety of responsibilities and duties, you'll get that with police work. This can be especially true with new officers, when one of the key purposes behind the assignments they are given is to expose them to different aspects of police work, both inside the station and outside on the streets. Alternating between night shifts and day shifts, at any point in time you could find yourself directing traffic, monitoring the crowd at a rock concert, guarding a criminal suspect who is hospitalized—or guarding the front desk at the station house.

Once you have gone through basic training and become a full-fledged member of the force, you'll most likely start out as a patrol officer. While small police departments will naturally command small numbers of patrol officers, in large departments these individuals make up the majority of the force. Patrol officers do exactly what their title implies: patrol a designated area, usually by car or on foot, and in some cases by motorcycle or even on horseback.

JUST THE FACTS
The first-ever motorcycle cop came on the scene in 1909 in Pittsburgh, Pennsylvania. Vehicle of choice: a Harley.

The overall role of a police officer is to protect people and property, maintain order, and enforce the law, always within the scope of safeguarding every citizen's constitutional rights. Toward that goal, you'll be trained as an officer to watch for and investigate suspicious situations, illegal activities and public safety hazards. When you're on patrol, this can run the gamut from spotting driving and parking violations, reporting traffic lights that aren't working, to responding to radio calls that take you to the scene of serious incidents, either reported or in progress, such as burglaries, muggings, murders, domestic abuse, rapes and suicides.

MAKING THE SCENE

As an officer at a crime scene, you may need to identify and question suspects and witnesses, gather criminal evidence, and arrest and transport suspects to the police station for booking and detention. Depending on the nature of the crime, you may perform these duties at the direction of, or to assist, detectives also called to the scene. When suspects you've taken in are brought to trial, as the arresting officer you may be called upon to testify in court for the prosecuting attorney.

A large part of a police officer's job involves ensuring people's safety and maintaining order. As such, officers are often on hand for crowd and traffic control during large public gatherings—sporting events, parades, concerts, political rallies and the like. They are called on to perform similar services in emergency situations, such as fires, natural disasters and auto accidents, and are trained to provide basic medical care to aid accident or crime victims.

Police officers may work alone or with partners, often depending on the nature of a particular assignment or the size of the police force. Typically you'll work 40-hour weeks on rotating shifts. But you can plan on being "on call" night and day, weekends and holidays included. Plus, it's not unusual to work extra shifts and long hours because of department overload or during pressing criminal investigations.

THE BOTTOM LINE

What you'll earn as a police officer varies, of course, from force to force. On a national level, the Bureau of Labor Statistics reports that the median salary of nonsupervisory police officers was approximately $32,000 a year in 1992. Those in the middle 50 percent earned between about $24,500 and $41,200. Those at the lowest end (10 percent) were paid less than $18,400, while the highest paid (also 10 percent) made over $51,200 a year. Salaries tend to be higher in metropolitan areas with large police departments. But wherever you work, your salary can vary significantly based on the level of overtime pay.

Your compensation package as a police officer also includes standard employee benefits such as paid vacation days, sick leave, and health and life insurance. Most departments will supply you with required equipment—such as handcuffs and nightsticks—and provide special allowances for you to purchase uniforms. Generous pension plans are a major benefit of police work. Many officers are able to retire at half-pay after 20 or 25 years of service, free to pursue second careers or other interests while still in their 40s or 50s.

THE OTHER SIDE OF THE COIN

There are real advantages to the profession of policing. It offers you the chance to do responsible, worthwhile work. Each day holds the promise of making a positive difference in people's lives, right on up to saving lives. Other pluses include the variety of duties, the personal challenges you'll undergo and the flexible work schedules versus the 9–5 office routine. It's also a profession known for a spirit of camaraderie, where officers "take care of their own." On the practical side, the level of job security tends to be higher than that of many other occupations, not to mention the generally liberal salaries and benefits that come with the territory.

Then there are the tough parts of the job. You know that police work can be risky. But it's a different thing to actually experience the risks. You will face unruly crowds and criminals who can be angry, violent, armed

WHAT OFFICERS EARN

The information provided below is based on the Labor Relations Information System's 1992 Wage and Benefit Survey. The data represent an *average* of wages and benefits paid to officers in 322 cities nationwide with populations greater than 50,000. Keep in mind, therefore, that compensation may vary significantly among individual cities.

Average Monthly Wages
Police Officer (entry level)—$2,152
Sergeant—$3,442
Lieutenant—$3,914
Captain—$4,434
Chief—$5,981
Note: Figures listed (1) represent top level wages for each ranked position except police officer, and (2) do not include any additional wages paid for longevity on force.

Benefits
Health Insurance Contribution
- Percentage of full family premium paid by *employer*—90.37%
- Percentage of full family premium paid by *employee*—9.63%

Retirement Plan Contribution
- Percentage of salary paid toward plan by *employer*—16.26%
- Percentage of salary paid toward plan by *employee*—5.04%

Plainclothes Allowance
- $315/year

Holidays
- 86.6 hours/year

Vacation after 10 Years
- 142.2 hours/year

and irrational. The authority of your badge and the threat of your firearm may not be heeded. You won't have a stunt expert doubling for you in car chases like in the movies. Cars collide. The bullets are real. And again unlike the movies, the "good guys" don't always win.

SERIOUS BUSINESS

Doing this job means living in harm's way and dealing with human tragedies. That's true whether you're an urban cop or a rural cop, and whether your brushes with violent crime and tragic events are frequent or rare. But it's not only the potential dangers of the job that can take their toll. Both substance-abuse problems and incidents of domestic violence are cropping up among officers at many departments. According to findings from a three-year study released by the New York City Police Department in 1993, police officers are more than twice as likely to commit suicide than people in the general population. Those findings say a lot about the stresses of the job, which can come from many directions.

JUST THE FACTS
Police officers are often referred to as "The Thin Blue Line"—the protective force positioned between law-abiding citizens on one side, and criminals and dangerous forces on the other.

Try to imagine the level of frustration officers experience when they collar a criminal for rape or murder, are backed by an army of witnesses to testify against him—yet watch the guy go free on a technicality or a plea bargain. Try to picture—and later erase—the image of a 3-year-old child who has just been brutally beaten or sexually abused by a parent. Try to grasp the sense of betrayal and disappointment at learning about fellow officers being under arrest for taking bribes or selling drugs. Even the most skilled and diligent police officers can find it difficult to cope with those kinds of emotions. Because such feelings are not easy to put aside when the shift ends, extra pressures can be brought to the home front as well.

Other aspects of policing can generate more subtle levels of stress. Patrolling the same daily beat has its tedious side, both when there's no action on the streets and when you're dealing with the same kind of action time after time. The routine paperwork, reports to file and bureaucratic red tape can become equally grueling. On the personal level, the downside of a changing schedule and lots of overtime is that these can disrupt your sleeping habits, family life and social life.

THE IMAGE

One of the more taxing elements of policing has to do with public perceptions. That can mean high expectations—living up to the image of an officer as a superhuman being, always calm, cool and collected, never making mistakes. Or it can mean hostility—dealing with people who blame cops for rising crime or hold the firm opinion that all cops are corrupt, racist and power-hungry. And it's not just criminal suspects who can be belligerent. Even normally reasonable people can fly into a rage when they're a victim or perpetrator of a crime.

Police are also under intense scrutiny from the press and are frequently subjected to news reports on crooked cops, rogue cops and department-wide scandals. In 1995, a police officer in New Orleans was charged with the murders of three people, one of them another officer. A group of New York City officers made national headlines for their lewd and disorderly conduct at the hotel they were staying at during a police convention. Officers in Philadelphia pleaded guilty to planting drug evidence, stealing money and falsifying arrest reports. And is there anybody out there who hasn't heard of Detective Mark Fuhrman? These kind of stories not only are demoralizing to "good cops," but all too often have the effect of smearing the profession rather than just the lone offenders.

Those are some of the tough parts of policing. They are important factors for you to be aware of and consider when making a move to join the force. But consider, too, the kind of help and support that's available once you're there. Many police departments actively provide the kind of training and assistance officers need to effectively handle the pressures of police work, including stress management programs and confidential counseling services. Fellow officers can be a source of understanding and encouragement. Also on your side is the fact that plenty of citizens out there respect and are grateful for the work that police officers do. As virtually every person in this field will tell you with conviction—the majority of cops are good cops.

THE APPLICATION PROCESS

If what you've read so far appeals to you, and you think you've got the "right stuff" to be a police officer, it's time to think about what's involved in applying for the job.

DEFENDING THE DEFENDERS

Gilbert Gallegos, president of the National Fraternal Order of Police, made the following statements in his article on "Racism in Law Enforcement" in the wake of the O.J. Simpson trial and related events. (The full article appeared in the October issue of *Newswatch*, an FOP publication.) The Fraternal Order of Police (FOP) is the largest police organization in the world, with more than 270,000 members.

"Mark Fuhrman—an enigma or the norm? During the past two months citizens and members of the media have asked that question of me often.

My response has been that Fuhrman and others like him are not representative of the vast number of professional police officers that I know. He, and others like him, do not represent the spirit and dedication of the 270,000 members of the Fraternal Order of Police.

While the numbers of racist cops are minute among the more than 600,000 professionals throughout the country, those few cause problems for all of us. The vast majority of hard working officers are conscientious, fair minded and dedicated to the principles of justice and service to the community. After all, we live in the communities we serve. . . .

While law enforcement has taken many hits during the past few months—Waco, Ruby Ridge, the O.J. trial—we cannot lower our heads in shame. We must lift our heads with pride because of the service we continue to provide to citizens despite race or creed, rich or poor. Our efforts should be to right the wrongs and to continue serving the public we swore to protect."

The basic requirements you need to be aware of include:

- A minimum age, usually between 18 and 21, and a maximum ranging from 29 to 40
- Excellent health and good vision
- U.S. citizenship, or in some cities, resident alien status
- A high school diploma or its equivalent
- A valid driver's license for the state

- A clean criminal record

In Chapter 6 you'll find the specifics of how police officers are selected. But briefly, here's what you can expect:

- A written test
- A thorough medical exam
- Various tests of physical ability
- A psychological test or personality evaluation

YOUR COMPETITIVE EDGE

Since police departments frequently have more applicants than job openings, they pay attention to "extra" abilities or experiences that make you stand out from the crowd. Beyond meeting the basic requirements for becoming a police officer, having qualifications in these areas may help your cause:

- *Education:* Many departments have adopted or are moving toward higher educational standards for police recruits. Educational level has already been linked to *rank promotions* at several departments, for example, New York City and Chicago. Most experts in the field believe that it's just a matter of time before a college degree becomes a minimum requirement across the country for *entry* to the force. This isn't yet the case, but as a rule of thumb there's an advantage in having completed at least some college (including junior colleges and universities); more of an advantage for earning a college degree in any field; and a greater advantage still in having taken courses or earned a degree in a directly relevant field such as police science, law enforcement or criminal justice.
- *Second Languages:* Being able to speak more than one language can also be an unofficial "plus." This is especially true in urban areas with large ethnic populations, where knowing Spanish, Korean or Filipino could all come in handy depending on the neighborhood. Being able to communicate with non-English-speaking people in their native languages can help enormously in resolving disputes, directing crowds, aiding crime victims and conducting investigations. Most important, it also could save your life in certain threatening situations.
- *Computer Skills:* Knowing how to type on a keyboard is a major asset. Understanding even the basics about computers is even better. High-tech communications systems are becoming more and more a part of police work, right down to patrol officer duties. For example, a patrol car equipped with a mobile digital terminal or notebook computer may allow officers to tap into state or national data bases to run driver, vehicle, weapon and record checks, or to send inquiries via electronic mail ("e-mail"). Completing routine reports on a computer can also save a lot of time. When computers are networked or linked to a mainframe at the department, this "paperwork" can then go directly into department "files" for storage.

- Drug testing and possibly a polygraph (lie detector) test
- A thorough background investigation
- An oral interview with one officer or a board of police officers and citizens

JUST THE FACTS
Over 90 percent of local police departments in the U.S. have fewer than 50 officers on their force. About half have fewer than 10 officers.

Those are the basics of what's involved in applying for the job. You also need to be aware that the competition for police jobs tends to be steep. For example, in 1994, 6,000 people applied to become police officers in Philadelphia, Pennsylvania; 8,000 applied in Fort Worth, Texas; and a grand total of 57,366 applied in New York City. Compared to the number of new full-time officer jobs filled that same year, Philadelphia hired one in 20; Fort Worth hired one in 80; New York City hired one in 21. (Note also that new hires don't always come from current applications, but instead may be based on an eligibility list of applicants from previous years.)

The good news is that overall job prospects in the field are favorable. There are roughly 600,000 police officers in the U.S. today and the U.S. Bureau of Labor Statistics (BLS) projects that employment of police officers will be on the rise through the year 2005. Plus, if you look at population statistics, sheer numbers are on your side: over the next ten years, there will simply be fewer people in the 18-21 age group that makes up the majority of police applicants. Fewer people means a smaller pool of recruits.

You can rest assured that the demand for top-notch candidates is strong at police departments across the country. To join the ranks, you'll need to show yourself as someone who's willing and able to perform beyond the call of duty—exactly the kind of recruit that every department is looking for. The more you know about what goes into the selection of recruits, the better you can prepare yourself to fit the bill.

MOVING UP AND AROUND

Leap ahead for a minute. You've passed the entrance requirements at your department of choice. You've gone through all the police officer training and really learned the ropes. You've been on the force for awhile and proven yourself a commendable officer. Now where can you go from there?

To get some idea of where you can take your career as a police officer, you first need to have some notion of how police departments are organized. Police departments have many things in common in the way they're managed and operated: they have similar goals, serve similar functions, abide by similar laws and are mostly all run under local city government and control. However, no single organizational chart fits every single police department.

That's mostly a matter of size. For example, it's typical to organize departments by breaking them down into divisions that are each responsible for a specific type of police work. The larger the department, the more divisions you'll find. In fact, the number of *divisions* on a large force is usually greater than the total number of *officers* in a small department. If you join a rural police force, your department may have no formal divisions at all—among other differences from a large urban force (see sidebar on next two pages).

In a department that is organized by divisions, patrol officers generally make up one division. Other divisions carry names that are probably familiar to you

POLICING IN RURAL TERRITORY

On a big city police force, you could be one of a thousand, ten thousand, or more than twenty thousand sworn officers. At the other extreme, you could be one of 10 officers or less as an officer serving a rural community. Along with answering to a much smaller roll call, outlined below are some of the differences you'd find working on a rural force. (Note that small departments aren't necessarily rural, although some of the same characteristics may apply.)

The Daily Routine
Rural departments won't have all the specialized divisions of policing that a large force has. A rural officer tends to be more of a jack-of-all-trades, responsible for all different types of police work. Because overall crime rates are lower in rural communities, especially the level of violent crime, officers there face relatively less danger on a day-to-day basis. The pace is slower—and the standard of living generally higher—than in an urban environment. Rural officers also work directly with their superior officers (including the chief of police being right at hand) and tend to get more personal guidance and instruction as a result. Working closely with just a few fellow officers makes good teamwork essential. It also makes for less bureaucracy and fewer "layers of management" to wade through to make decisions and get the job done.

Tools of the Trade
Limited operating budgets are common among rural departments. This can result in a force being under-staffed. It often means less access to new or more sophisticated equipment and systems. And there may not be funds available to invest in officers through continued training and educational programs. (Take note, however, that the same can be true of large forces that have gotten the budget ax. In turn, rural departments in communities with a high tax base may have all the latest, greatest equipment at their disposal.)

Adapting to the Territory
Rural and urban officers alike handle criminal matters such as property crimes, juvenile offenses and domestic violence. But some kinds of criminal activity are unique to certain rural areas, such as illegal game or fish poaching; thefts of farm crops, livestock or timber; or illegal immigration in border regions. Officers in most rural areas may deal less with cocaine and crack dealers, but instead may have to contend with liquor and tobacco trafficking or marijuana crops being grown and distributed. Regarding crimes related to sub-stance abuse, alcohol is the drug that represents more of a problem throughout rural communities, espe-cially incidents of DUI (driving under the influence) and DWI (driving while intoxicated).

The Familiarity Factor
Police officers in rural areas tend to know or recognize the people involved in a crime. Likewise, the vic-tims, witnesses and perpetrators of crimes are more likely to be acquainted with each other. This level of familiarity can help officers identify and track suspects in a criminal investigation. Yet it can create a unique

(continued)

set of problems as well. Victims and witnesses in a small town may be less apt to press charges or point the finger at people they come into contact with on a regular basis. Rural officers, too, may find themselves having to investigate or arrest a local citizen who happens to be their neighbor's grandson, the upstanding local bank president, or their children's school teacher. Because of this "familiarity factor," rural officers often take a more personal approach and use less formal (but no less professional) procedures when conducting police business.

and are related to the nature of the crimes investigated—homicide, burglary, traffic, and vice and narcotics, to name a few. Still other divisions are responsible for the administrative side of police work, such as internal affairs, personnel, records, and training.

The organizing of the organization may not stop there. Especially in medium and large departments, divisions may be grouped and operated under another organizational unit known as a "bureau." The vice and narcotics division, for instance, could be part of the investigative services bureau; patrol could be part of the field services bureau; and internal affairs could be part of the administrative services bureau.

Many police departments—and definitely those in large urban areas—operate highly specialized divisions or bureaus. These may be in charge of functions that are unique or appropriate to specific geographical locations, such as a harbor patrol, an aviation unit, or mounted police. Or they may perform functions that are necessary because of a high level of community need surrounding certain types of criminal activity, such as bomb squads, hostage negotiations, sex crime analysis or juvenile services.

When you're checking out various police departments you may want to join, be aware that different departments may use slightly different titles for their various divisions and bureaus. The homicide and robbery division in one place may be called the "crimes against persons" division in another, just as an inves-

tigative services bureau may be referred to less formally as the detective bureau.

CAREER MOVES

It's clear that not all police forces are the same size or organized the same way. That being the case, you can assume that the opportunities for you to move up and around—to climb the ranks or try out different areas of police work—also won't be the same at every department. But some general guidelines do apply.

When it comes to "moving up," police departments tend to be more similar because the job titles used to show your rank or seniority on the force (sergeant, captain, etc.) are fairly standard everywhere. The differences between departments in this area have more to do with how many slots there are to fill, rather than with the types of promotions available. Where there are fewer slots to move up to, salary hikes may be awarded instead.

"Moving around" is another story. On a small force you won't do as much moving around the department because there simply won't be as many divisions to move around to; here you're more likely to be handling all kinds of police work on a regular basis. In bigger departments it's possible to do more moving around and concentrate on specific kinds of police work because that's where you can transfer in and out of specialized divisions.

The accompanying chart (see "Career Ladder Chart," opposite) gives you a look at how your career could progress within a large department based on rank. Going by job title alone, some positions obviously are higher in the pecking order—for example, a captain ranks higher than a sergeant. In addition, job titles may be assigned numerical rankings—such as Detective I, II or III—to recognize a higher level of authority, experience and expertise.

Keep in mind, of course, that a police force with a total of nine officers requires far fewer layers of command than those shown on the chart. And these exact career routes may not apply to every large or even medium-sized department. What the "ladder" in this particular chart shows is a *common* chain of command.

What isn't shown on the chart is that at each level of command, the position you hold may be further classified based on the division you work in or your area of assignment—for example, Homicide Detective, Records Division Sergeant, Precinct Captain, or Identification and Records Commander. This kind of job classification would be used to identify not only your rank on the force, but also the types of duties you perform as part of a certain division. Even officers with the same rank can have very different job duties.

For example, as a *Patrol Division Lieutenant*, your duties could range from conducting a roll call of the patrol force, to inspecting police logbooks for conformance with regulations, to setting bail for prisoners held on nonfelony charges.

As a *Traffic Lieutenant*, however, you would be focused on traffic control activities, such as directing officers to remove illegally parked vehicles; recommending changes in traffic control devices and regulations in the community; and working with organizers of a parade to determine police staffing requirements, traffic rerouting plans and crowd control procedures.

Yet as a *Community Relations Lieutenant*, you would have another focus altogether, performing duties such as supervising police personnel in efforts to resolve community social problems; working with social service agencies to develop crime prevention programs; and lecturing to local civic, school and community groups about the mission, functions and resources of the police department.

MOVING UP

You can see that what you'll be doing in different jobs depends on a number of factors—most of all, on your rank and division and the department's size and operating structure. Still, if you're moving up the ladder, you can count on certain changes taking place. For one thing, you're likely to take on a supervisory role, guiding the work of other police personnel. You'll probably have more administrative responsibilities, such as maintaining budgets, filing inspection reports, or conducting job performance evaluations of officers under your charge. Because moving up implies that you've gained a certain level of know-how about the department and the community it serves, you may become more involved in strategic planning and in setting department policies and goals. You'll also have more decision-making authority about matters of procedure, disciplinary measures, expenditures and so forth.

To become eligible for promotion, officers typically must go through a probationary period. How long the probationary period is depends on an individual department's promotion policy and personnel needs, but you can figure around three years on average—sometimes more, sometimes less. Plan on taking a written exam for promotion to sergeant, lieutenant and

CAREER LADDER CHART

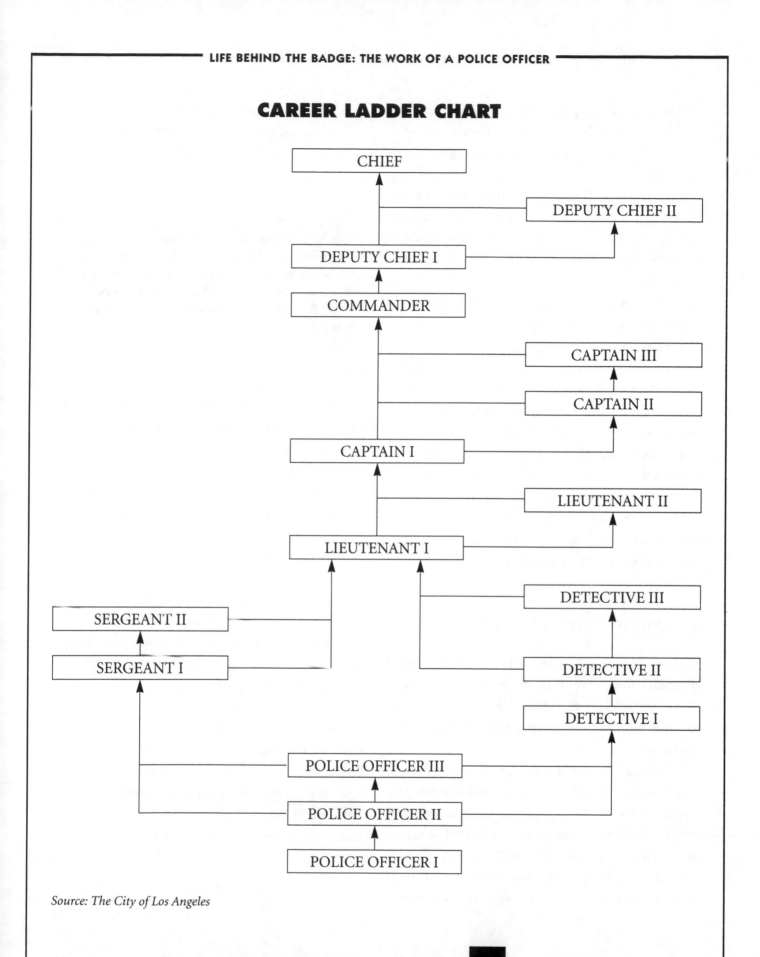

Source: The City of Los Angeles

captain; exam scores plus a record of your on-the-job performance then determine your placement on a promotion list. If you need additional training or education to advance, many police departments are willing to foot part or all of the bill. This could include tuition for you to take college courses or work toward a degree in a law enforcement-related field, often with an added incentive of boosting your salary if you end up earning the degree.

When you're thinking about how far you can go in a police organization, remember that moving up the ladder doesn't necessarily equal greater job satisfaction. Some officers aspire to one day occupy the police chief's office. Others feel at their best patrolling the beat. Once you're on the force, it will be up to you to decide where you want to go and to prove yourself capable of getting there. One of the best things you can do is take the initiative to learn new skills and knowledge and tackle different assignments. The more time you spend on the job, the better you'll be able to tell what kind of police work appeals to you most. Then you can navigate your career path accordingly.

CHANGING WITH THE TIMES

Back before automobiles and radio transmitters, you'd most likely find police officers either at the precinct station or out walking their beat. They were a fixture in the neighborhood; they knew the people and the people knew them.

Naturally, many things have changed over the years. One major shift occurred when foot patrol gave way to car patrol, allowing officers to cover more territory during their watch and to reach crime scenes faster. Patrol cars were also a visible and constant reminder of police presence, which was viewed in and of itself as a crime control strategy. The now common

"911" dispatching system produced another shift in policing when it came along with its promise that the police were just a phone call away.

JUST THE FACTS
Back in 1895, the New York City Police Department formed a bicycle squad to slow down horse-drawn carriages. The two-wheeling, 29-officer squad made 1,366 arrests for speeding that year alone.

Go back for a moment to the example of how the patrol car influenced policing, but this time consider the downside. The simple act of being inside instead of outside a car separates an officer from people on the street. Yet these are people who might have vital information, valid complaints and some good suggestions about how to reduce crime in their communities.

Think, too, of certain disadvantages of the 911 system. Besides being subject to overload and non-emergency reports, the system puts officers in a *reactive* position—constantly responding to calls about crimes that may or may not be in progress by the time they arrive. As a result, the chances of apprehending a criminal, much less preventing a crime, are reduced. According to research reported by John E. Eck and William Spelman in "Problem Solving: Problem-Oriented Policing" in *Newport News*, less than 5 percent of all 911 calls in most cities bring an officer to a crime in progress, where he or she can intercede or make an arrest. In fact, the majority of 911 calls—anywhere from 50 to 90 percent—are not even about crime.

Another familiar strategy with some clear drawbacks is that of policing "by the numbers." That's where your performance as an officer would be evaluated by the number of calls you've answered, arrests you've made or tickets you've issued, or even how many times you manage to circle a neighborhood in your patrol car during a shift. Needless to say, a whole lot more can enter into the question of whether or not you're doing a good job.

It's not that these and other common police procedures need to be thrown out the window altogether. But some of the weaknesses in these systems began to surface as early as the 1960s. At the same time that police departments were being expanded and loads of new equipment were being purchased, crime rates went on the rise and citizens began to express greater levels of fear. Something wasn't working.

IN THE SPOTLIGHT

The 1960s launched a time of major social upheaval and unrest. Decades of deeply imbedded prejudices were being brought to the surface. Authority was being questioned. When it came to civil rights issues, the anti-war movement and the corruption of government officials, police were often caught in the middle. They weren't used to the level of "civil disobedience" happening around them, nor the level of disrespect that came with being viewed as part of "the Establishment." Suddenly their job was putting them in direct confrontation with large groups of citizens. Their methods of policing were being grilled in the media and by the public. Meanwhile, they were trying to absorb and adapt to the changes in society just like everyone else. You could argue that people's expectations of the police were unrealistically high.

FIGHTING PREJUDICE INSIDE THE FORCE

Efforts to stamp out racist and sexist attitudes among police officers are on the rise and receive a lot of attention in the press. Now another form of discrimination is being heeded by an organization known as Law Enforcement Gays and Lesbians (LEGAL) International. The organization was formed to help gay and lesbian law enforcement officers overcome the particular issues and challenges they face on the job relative to their sexual orientation.

LEGAL International's membership includes various law enforcement professions (police officers, state patrol, corrections, court officials). Its first annual convention was held in September, 1995 during a conference in Los Angeles that was co-sponsored by the Los Angeles Police Department and the Golden State Peace Officers Association (GSPOA), a California-based group of gay and lesbian police officers and sheriffs. At the LEGAL convention, 115 police departments were represented from 26 U.S. states as well as 5 other countries: Canada, Germany, Denmark, Australia and Great Britain.

For further information, contact: LEGAL International, P.O. Box 1161, Old Chelsea Station, New York, NY, 10011-1161.

But from the people's point of view, if the police couldn't keep the peace, then who would?

The complicated issues and problems that were raised over three decades ago live on today in one form or another, along with a variety of modern offshoots. That's why the methods and goals of policing have been put under the microscope for close inspection. Slowly but surely, changes are underway. It's showing up in what the public is asking for from police departments across the country. And it's showing up in how police officers are being trained, in the demographic make-up of departments, and in the roles and responsibilities officers are being asked to take on.

Police departments today are focused on matching their tactics to the times. And despite the obvious addition of high-speed cruisers and high-tech tools, some of the current changes in policing look suspi-

ciously like "the good ol' days" when officers walked their beat.

TRENDS AND OPPORTUNITES

Certain major forces or trends are driving change in both the mission and methods of modern policing. Since you're a potential police recruit, it's important to be aware of these forces. What's happening in policing now—and where it's headed—have a lot to do with your future in this profession.

One of these driving forces won't come as a surprise: the public has issued a mandate to *get tough on crime*. Another major force is directly linked to the first: police departments are aware of the need to *get back in touch* with the communities they serve. Both these

AN OUNCE OF PREVENTION

Keeping kids in line has become a major focus of policing due to rising national rates of juvenile crime. U.S. Attorney General Janet Reno has projected that teenage crime will double by the year 2010. Increases in violent crime among teenagers are especially disturbing—the murder rate alone rose 165 percent from 1985 to 1993 among teenagers between the ages of 14 to 17.

It's a complicated problem without simple solutions. But among the various approaches being tried, juvenile crime *prevention programs* have been gaining ground. In 1995, the National Recreation and Park Association issued findings from a nationwide study indicating that recreation and training programs can have a major impact on reducing rates of juvenile crime and arrests. Experiments at many police departments support these findings on a local level. For example:

- A 26% decline in juvenile arrests reported by the Dallas (Texas) Police Department in 1995 was attributed to a gang-intervention program begun five years earlier. The program combined a series of youth education, recreation and job-training initiatives and was sponsored by 17 civic organizations.
- Similar results—a 27% drop in juvenile crime—were reported by the Fort Myers (Florida) Police Department after three years of running its STARS program, which focuses on academics, sports and cultural activities. The academic effect was dramatic: as of 1995, 75% of the city's youths had a C grade average or better, versus only 25% before the program began.

trends affect the demand for police officers—and the demands being placed on officers.

Getting tough on crime centers on the fact that crime is a hot topic, one of the most serious social issues of the day. It's encouraging that some areas of the country have seen a decline in criminal activity in recent years. But when you look at the big picture, crime rates have risen steadily over the last thirty years and remain critically high. As a result, the public's cry for more police officers is ringing out loud and strong.

The U.S. Justice Department's Bureau of Justice Statistics (BJS) revealed a whopping 43,622,000 crimes in 1993—these being crimes reported, not all crimes actually committed. In the news daily are accounts of robberies, assaults, rapes, murders, drug-related crime and gang-related crime. The incidence of violent crime is especially alarming: according to the BJS, violent crime is behind the conviction of 94% of state prisoners, many of whom are repeat offenders.

The general trend in lawmaking leans toward harsher sentencing in the courts, but it's slow going. Mostly due to overcrowded prisons and courtrooms, plea bargaining has become commonplace, which results in large numbers of known criminal offenders being released on parole or probation. Some wind up becoming law-abiding citizens. Many don't. That's another reason for the current clamor for good police officers—and more of 'em.

Wanting, of course, doesn't always mean getting. Funds aren't always available to increase the size of any given police force. In addition, research conducted in the 1970s and 1980s pointed to the fact that having more officers doesn't automatically mean having less crime. Other elements have to change as well. So along with hiring extra officers when they need to and can, many police departments are testing new methods of policing that focus on preventing crime, not just nabbing criminals after the fact.

Back to the Beat

That leads around to the need for police departments to get back in touch with the communities they serve. The way many departments are doing this is by adopting a strategy known as *community policing.* (Problem-oriented policing, strategic policing, neighborhood policing and back-to-the-beat policing are other names used to refer to this or other strategies based on a similar philosophy.)

Giving more of a leadership role to patrol officers is a key element of community policing. According to supporters of this strategy, that's just common sense. Patrol officers are out in the community 24 hours a day, every day of the week. They have the closest contact with citizens' concerns and criminal activity on the street. So, the argument goes, if you're a patrol officer, naturally you should have some say in how departments go about enforcing the law and controlling crime.

Patrol officers now are being encouraged to do more than issue citations, make arrests and hand in reports. They are being asked to use their first-hand knowledge of crime and related problems in the community to help develop solutions that work.

A Call for Teamwork

Community policing also asks patrol officers to seek the help of local citizens in keeping the peace. This takes getting to know the people on your beat—residents, store owners, church groups, schools. It takes an effort to learn about people's fears and complaints and their ideas for creating a safer community. And it takes time to develop a partnership with citizens and earn their trust. For example, instead of always being assigned to different beats, you may be regularly patrolling the same beat—by car and on foot—so that you become a familiar face to the people who live and work there. That's the aspect of community policing that looks a lot like the good ol' days. As you become a part of the neighborhood, you have more of a stake in making things better.

Cities across the country—Houston, Chicago, Tampa, San Diego and many more—have spent the last several years doing what it takes to put this strategy into action. The models they've developed are now making their way into departments in smaller cities and towns. The shift to community or problem-oriented policing isn't an overnight process. Police resources have to be used in different ways. Often more officers are needed, especially when increased foot patrol is part of the plan. Most of all, a shift in mindset has to take place. Community policing calls for more teamwork at all levels of the department. It puts the focus on cleaning up neighborhoods and attacking crime at its roots, not just treating the symptoms through one-at-a-time responses to 911 calls. And it includes sharing responsibility and working together with citizens to achieve these goals.

These goals are also being supported by many other actions on the part of police departments. The technical skills, interpersonal skills and the philosophy behind community policing are now being incorporated into police officer training programs—both for new recruits and long-time officers. Departments are also taking advantage of advancements in technology. Sophisticated high-tech equipment is being used increasingly to help control crime, solve crimes and work more effectively with other police departments and government agencies. In addition, departments are boosting their efforts to bring more women and members of diverse racial and ethnic groups onto the force, changing the traditional white male image of the police force to better reflect the demographic make-up of the population they serve.

All of this influences your career as a police officer because it spells new opportunities. Think about it. Once you join the force, you'll start off as a patrol officer. Modern policing strategies value and rely on the patrol officer. How well an officer deals one-on-one with people on the street can make or break the goals of community policing. That's where your opportunities come in.

To wage a successful battle against crime, police departments need qualified, committed recruits more than ever before. They need your ability to be a leader, a problem-solver, a negotiator, a decision-maker, a role model, a team-player and an independent thinker. Yes, the traditional chain of command still exists. No, the bureaucracy hasn't vanished. But the current trends in policing are designed to elevate both the role of the officer on patrol and the profession of policing as a whole.

Making the Commitment

The widespread and deep-seated problems of modern society make this an especially challenging time to be a police officer. You'll need a good dose of idealism and optimism about the ability of the police to enforce the law and clean up the streets. Add to that a realistic point of view about some of the difficulties you'll face in carrying out those tasks. No matter how well they do their job, police officers simply can't right all of society's wrongs. But as one old saying goes, if you're not part of the problem, you're part of the solution. Being a good cop is definitely part of the solution.

Now you need to get there from here. Set your course. Make your plan. Get yourself ready. Luckily, many paths are open for you to learn more about the profession and prepare yourself to become a top candidate for the force. To start you off in that direction, here are some actions you can take.

1. *Get fit.* If you're currently dedicated to a regular physical fitness program, that's great. Keep it up. If not, then now's the time to start. Most police departments include a physical performance test in the application process. You can ask in advance

about what's involved—sit-ups, dummy drags, wall climbs, stair running and so on. In general, know that you'll be tested for strength, agility, quickness and endurance. Tip: If you're not already doing so, you could get a head start by enrolling in martial arts classes. These disciplines are valuable not only for their practical techniques of self-defense, but also for the "mind/body connection," which is a valuable tool for remaining centered and focused under stressful circumstances.

2. *Do some networking.* The best resource for "telling it like it is" and helping you take the right steps are people now working in the field. Maybe you have family or friends or acquaintances involved in policing as officers or educators. Maybe you'll need to make some contacts on your own. In either case, it's a good idea to seek people out who have some first-hand knowledge. You can ask questions and get some helpful pointers. You might even make some friends on the force you end up wanting to join. The point is not about getting any special treatment—you'll have to pass all the same tests that any other applicant must pass. It's about getting information that you can factor into your decisions and actions toward becoming a police officer.

3. *Conduct your own background investigation.* Along with talking to people in the field, mix in plenty of reading. Many police organizations and government agencies publish newsletters that are available to non-members. The criminal justice departments of colleges and universities are another source for newsletters, academic papers, research reports and books. You may want to subscribe to various police magazines or review them at public or college libraries (note: they're not always available at newsstands). Also keep up to date through newspaper articles—not only about the police profession itself, but about social issues, legal issues

and new laws, crime trends and other areas that directly influence police work. If you have access to a computer and can get on the Internet, you'll find a wealth of material on policing, including data provided by and about individual police departments. Plus, you can join any number of on-line "discussion" groups and extend your networking contacts electronically.

4. *Research police departments you may want to join.* You'll be doing part of this homework if you focus some of your reading and networking efforts on individual departments. You'll also need to contact departments you're considering directly, by phone, mail and/or a personal visit. Think through ahead of time the kind of basic facts you want to find out about a department—such as how many officers are on the force, how it's organized, what kind of opportunities it offers. Very important are the specifics about a department's entry requirements. You need to know in advance, for example, about residential and educational requirements in case meeting those would involve relocating or getting additional schooling. Tip: Research forces of different sizes and in different locales. Even if you already think you know where you want to go, the people you meet and the information you get from another kind of place may just change your mind. There's also no substitute for "good vibes"—when you visit a place and it just feels right for you.

5. *Find out when and how you can apply.* By this point you'll already know the entry requirements for the department(s) you are considering. But you'll need to get a date, time and location for taking the written exam. And you'll need to know what's next after you take the test. For example, if a department doesn't have immediate hiring needs, then once you pass the exam you might be put on an eligibility list and contacted later to move for-

SURFING THE BEAT

One way to gather a variety of information about law enforcement and the profession of policing—and boost your computer skills at the same time—is to hook up to the Internet and start searching (commonly known as "surfing") the World Wide Web.

The Internet was created just a few years back as a defense project and has since become the world's largest computer network. Through the Internet you can access the World Wide Web, a multimedia application that combines video, graphics, text and sound. On the Web you'll find over 50,000 specific "sites" sponsored by numerous organizations and individuals. Among these are Web sites linking you to police departments, law enforcement agencies and other related resources across the U.S. and around the globe.

Listed below are a few sites worth checking out. Reaching these sites is just like finding someone's house—you need to know the address to get there. That's what is known as a "URL address" on the Web, also provided below for these sites. But each is only a starting point for your investigation. Once you've arrived at the main address, you can surf into a vast collection of other sites.

- *Cop Net & Police Resource List.* The premiere site for police-specific data. The most notable feature of Cop Net is that it gives you access to individual police departments. No two sites are identical, but most offer key background information and contact names. Included are "links" to city/county/state police departments, campus police departments, U.S. federal government agencies, military agencies, international agencies, commercial sites, and diverse public information and law enforcement association sites. (Note: Cop Net also features a private "Officers-Only Area" which you can tap into *after* you join the force and can get the password. . .) [URL address: http://police.sas.ab.ca]

- *Cecil Greek's Criminal Justice Page.* You'll be greeted with a picture of Alcatraz when you enter this site, which was created by a professor of criminal justice at the University of Southern Florida. Along with law enforcement sites (you can also get to Cop Net from here), there are links to judicial and legal sites, corrections/penal sites, education sites and various on-line magazines—called "e-zines" on the Web. An assortment of subjects are covered, such as current court cases, drugs and alcohol, terrorism, juvenile delinquency, and the death penalty. While you're there, you can check out the Most Wanted List, trial photos and, if you have a taste for the grotesque, actual forensic photos. [URL address: http://www.stpt.usf.edu/~greek/cj.html]

- *Law Enforcement Sites on the Web.* This site was developed by a licensed peace officer who has taught at the Lamar University Institute of Technology and the Criminal Justice Training Center's Regional Police Academy in Beaumont, Texas. It is billed as "possibly the largest collection of law enforcement sites on the Web." That's the plus side—all the other sites you can access from here. However, precisely because it's so thorough, it can be time-consuming to work with. A search function helps, allowing you to confine your travels by giving key words (such as "police") that describe your particular interests. [URL address: http://www.geopages.com/CapitolHill/1814/ira.html]

(continued)

- **Office of International Criminal Justice.** You can explore the field of criminal justice worldwide from this site, which is organized by the following categories: Publications, Training, Conferences, Consulting Services and Other Criminal Justice Sites. The three "e-zine" publications featured here make for some good reading with their on-line articles about policing and other law enforcement topics. *CJ The Americas On-Line* covers the U.S. plus other North American and South American countries. Also available are *CJ International* and *CJ Europe*. [URL address: http://www.acsp.uic.edu/index.html]

- **U.S. Federal Government Agencies.** Each branch of the federal government and every federal agency are covered here—the Departments of Justice, Defense, Labor and all the rest, as well as federal courts, independent agencies and other government indexes. You can also get to Congress and the White House for information about current legislative activity, transcripts of speeches, and other data. And if you've got an opinion you'd like to express, you can even send messages to the President and Vice President. [URL address: http://www.lib.lsu.edu/gov/fedgov.html]

In addition to Web sites, the Internet connects you to electronic mail (e-mail), USENET bulletin boards and electronic discussion groups. Through these services you can have on-line "conversations" with people in the field of law enforcement. Or you can simply read the many articles, press releases and other electronic notices that are posted—including postings about job opportunities and openings. Both the Internet and the Web can be sources of valuable information for your career. If you don't have your own computer, find out whether local libraries, colleges or commercial computer centers can get you connected.

---

ward with the other steps in the applicant testing process. The personnel or recruiting division is usually the right place to contact for these details. Also ask about anything you may need to bring with you to the exam—for instance, pencils, notepads, a pocket calculator, paperwork or documents (such as photo identification, a birth certificate or a social security card). Keep in mind departments can vary widely as to how often they give exams, anywhere from four times a week to once every two years.

6. **Prepare for the written exam.** It was mentioned earlier in this chapter that you don't need to know police regulations or the law of the land in order to take the entrance exam. But you can study and give yourself an advantage in other ways. In general, the written exam will gauge your skills in such areas as logical reasoning; good judgment;

problem-solving; observation and memory for details; basic grammar and writing skills; and reading comprehension. A multiple-choice format is typical. Questions often make use of police terms, procedures, scenarios and passages from actual police manuals or other such documents. All the information you need to answer the questions will be there; the key lies in how you interpret and respond to the information presented.

7. **Prepare for the oral interview.** Some people get intimidated at the idea of being quizzed about their background, skills and ambitions by seasoned police officers. It may help to think of it no differently than any other job interview. And it may help to practice. Spend some time alone thinking about your reasons for wanting to become a police officer. Think about your goals. Think about your particular knowledge, abilities and experience—what you can bring

to the force. Once you've spent some time thinking or even writing about these topics, enlist a colleague or family member (or a friend you've made on the force) to give you a "practice interview." Remember that you're not trying to come up with dry, rehearsed responses to any possible question. The "thinking" part is to get clear on your choice, your potential and your talents. The "practice" part is simply to get a feel for the interview situation. When it's time for the real interview, the best thing you can do is be yourself and be honest.

8. *Get involved in your community.* Explore opportunities in your community to learn about this profession by participating in police-sponsored activities. Volunteer work is a good bet in practically any community. One route is to join neighborhood crime-watch or clean-up groups that work in conjunction with local police precincts. Many departments sponsor juvenile sports and recreation programs, such as the Police Athletic League (PAL). The Police Explorers—Boy/Girl Scout troops sponsored by police departments—is another young people's program that often needs volunteers.

9. *Try out police work.* Local departments may have a Police Officer Reserve Program which would allow you to keep your regular job while committing time to working for the police department (something like the National Guard set-up). Or it may have internships available, either through the department or through a work/study arrangement with a college criminal justice program. Another possibility at some departments is a Police Cadet Corps program, which offers paid jobs to select college students between the ages of 18 and 21. Both internships and cadet programs give you the chance

to try your hand at various types of police work. Completing the latter, though, takes cadets straight to the police academy if they've met the required performance standards.

10. *Develop your competitive edge.* If you've delved into the above 9 steps with gusto, you definitely will have a competitive edge. But being the determined candidate that you are, you know there's always more you can do. In keeping with the previous sidebar "Your Competitive Edge," you can consider three more avenues for broadening your advantage. First, you could sign up for some college courses in police-related disciplines or other areas that you know would be useful for police work (such as classes in expository writing, psychology and sociology, or political science). Second, learn another language or take a refresher course in one you're already familiar with. (For this to really be of value, try to match your choice to the citizen population of the department.) Third, learn about computers. You could take a training class for popular software applications or just get yourself on a computer and learn by doing. With all three of these endeavors, it's important to set achievable goals for yourself and find appealing ways to meet them. You'll be more interested and engaged in the learning when the effort feels like something you *want* to do, not *have* to do.

Of course, at some point in the process of getting in shape, networking, investigating, preparing for tests, immersing yourself in the field and learning new skills... you'll just have to take the plunge. Make the commitment, apply for the job and show them what you've got.

C·H·A·P·T·E·R

THE WORK OF A STATE POLICE OFFICER

3

CHAPTER SUMMARY

To help you determine if you're ready to make the commitment to become a state police officer, this chapter gives you an overview of what being a trooper is all about. You'll learn about the specific duties and responsibilities of the job, what it's like to be out there every day, what kind of strengths and skills you need, what you can expect to be paid, the upsides—and downsides—of the job, and important issues and trends in the field. And you will get some tips on how to develop a competitive edge before you even start the application process.

The image of a state police officer is a strong one in the American imagination thanks to countless movies and TV series, from *CHiPs* to *Highway Patrol*, that portray troopers as tough, cool officers in high, shiny boots and impenetrable aviator sunglasses. The day-to-day reality of a state police officer's job, of course, is a lot less glamorous. But it *is* a tough job, requiring physical and mental agility, honesty and integrity, concern and dedication. And it *is* a cool job, because you're performing an important role in our society.

State police officers are known by a number of different names—including state troopers, highway patrol officers, and state traffic officers—and their roster of duties varies from state to state. But the major responsibility that state police officers across the country share is ensuring public safety on their state's roadways. This involves patrolling the highways, enforcing traffic laws, dealing with accidents and other emergencies, assisting motorists, and conducting safety programs.

In addition to highway responsibilities, state police in the majority of states also enforce criminal laws. In communities and counties that do not have a local police force or a large sheriff's department, state troopers are the primary law enforcement agents, investigating crimes such as burglary or assault. They may also help city or county police apprehend lawbreakers and control civil disturbances.

A full 80 percent of all state police forces in the country operated a special drug enforcement unit in 1993. The New York State Police, for example, offers Community Narcotics Enforcement Teams, making undercover troopers and investigators available to work with local law enforcement agencies. In 1992, its members worked with local police in Buffalo in an operation that led to the arrest of nearly 100 drug dealers and customers—one of the biggest roundups of street-level criminals in New York State history. (For specific duties related to state police officers, see sidebar on next page.)

All states except Hawaii have some type of statewide police force. Fourteen states, mostly in the west and south, have highway patrols, 27 have state police departments, and eight have departments of public safety.

JUST THE FACTS
The first modern statewide police agency was the Pennsylvania State Constabulary, established in 1905.

Demographics, Salary and Job Security

There were approximately 52,000 full-time sworn state police officers in the United States in 1993. This still tends to be a man's world—95 percent of these state officers were male. The force with the largest percentage of female troopers was the Wisconsin State Patrol, with 12.4 percent, followed by the Michigan State Police (9.7 percent) and the Florida Highway Patrol (9.4 percent). The North Carolina State Highway Patrol employed the least percentage of women (0.6 percent). State police forces also tend to be predominantly white. The average percent of white state police officers in 1993 was 89 percent; 7 percent were African American, 3 percent Hispanic, and 1 percent other races.

The pay of a state police officer varies widely, but on average, the base annual starting salary of an entry-level officer in 1993 was $23,300. The states paying the highest to troopers just starting out were Alaska ($42,192) and California ($35,016). The lowest-paying states were Vermont ($18,720) and Wyoming ($18,828). As far as benefits go, state troopers often get a package that includes such standard elements as vacation, sick leave, holiday, and overtime pay; insurance (life, medical and disability); a uniform allowance; tuition reimbursement; and a retirement plan.

Since the public sector, like so many other employers, has been "downsizing" in recent years, what's the job outlook for state police officers? The Bureau of Labor Statistics projects that the employment of all types

SPECIFIC DUTIES OF STATE TROOPERS

While the activities of state troopers vary from state to state, here are some of the specific duties they may be called on to perform:

- Patroling state and interstate highways
- Enforcing motor vehicle and criminal laws
- Monitoring traffic to: arrest or issue tickets or warnings to those violating motor vehicle regulations and safe driving practices, including speeding and driving while intoxicated; identify unsafe vehicles; detect stolen vehicles
- Providing information and assistance to motorists
- Observing and reporting public safety hazards, such as obstacles in the road or unsafe driving conditions
- Directing activities at the site of accidents or emergencies
- Providing first aid
- Investigating conditions and causes of accidents
- Directing traffic in congested areas
- Serving as escort for officials and dignitaries, funerals, processions, military convoys, parades
- Appearing in court as a witness in traffic violation and criminal cases
- Keeping records and making reports regarding activities, such as daily patrol occurrences or ongoing investigations
- Assisting law enforcement officers not under state jurisdiction
- Conducting safety programs for the public and at schools
- Inspecting automobiles and school buses for safe operating conditions
- Enforcing commercial vehicle weight laws
- Conducting driver exams

of police officers is expected to increase through the year 2005. An increasingly fearful society is demanding more police protection of all kinds. But employment growth will be tempered by continuing budgetary constraints faced by law enforcement agencies in many states. Turnover in police jobs is among the lowest of all occupations, and most job openings come from the need to replace retiring officers.

Rewards and Risks

State police officers, like other law enforcement officials, have one of the most challenging yet rewarding jobs in our society. State troopers serve the public in vital ways. They keep the highways safe from reckless or intoxicated drivers and make sure driving laws are obeyed. The skilled assistance they give when auto accidents or other emergencies occur can mean the difference between life and death. Each day brings a new set of situations to handle and encounters with a variety of people. Like their fellow officers in municipal police departments, state troopers are also known for having a great spirit of camaraderie. State troopers are enormously proud of the work they do, and strongly supportive of each other.

But there's another, darker side to the job of a state police officer. While most days are quiet "business as usual" times, there is always the threat of danger. Random acts of violence, fueled by ready access to guns and drugs, have become daily occurrences and number among the expected crimes that a state trooper must confront. High-speed car chases are certainly not the norm, but when they do occur there's the possibility of cars crashing and burning.

Unfortunately, the injury rate among law enforcement officers is higher than in many occupations and reflects the risks taken in pursuing speeding motorists, apprehending criminals and dealing with emergencies. And even when state police officers aren't directly in harm's way, they often have to perform duties that are difficult or unpleasant, such as confronting a driver under the influence of drugs or alcohol, or heartbreaking, like assisting at a bloody accident scene.

Stress is a way of life for the state police officer as well as for his/her family. And this stress comes from a number of sources—the danger inherent in this line of work; coping with everything from traffic jams to angry motorists to nasty weather; dealing with the perception of some citizens that law enforcement officials of all kinds are corrupt or racist. And since state troopers are as human as the next person, there is a tendency to take these tensions home, which can sometimes lead to additional problems.

It's important to think about this tough side of state policing if you plan to enter the field. But remember, too, that there's a lot of support available to help troopers handle the pressures of the job. Many departments sponsor training and counseling programs. You can also rely on fellow troopers support. They, better than anyone else, know how stressful state police work can be.

A DAY IN THE LIFE

Now that you have an idea of "the big picture," you probably want to know what it's like to be a state police officer on a day-to-day basis.

State police officers generally work a basic five-day, 40-hour week, with rotating shifts. Some states (New Jersey, for instance) use a "4/10" shift rotation—four days a week, 10 hours a day, which many troopers find better for their health and productivity. Since protection is needed on a 24-hour basis, you'll sometimes have to work nights, weekends and holidays. You may be required to work overtime, and you have to be prepared to be on call any time your services are needed.

Most troopers patrol the highways and byways of their states in cars and motorcycles, although some use planes, helicopters, and even boats. While you may be working with a partner, the great majority of state police (94 percent, according to a 1993 survey) go on patrol alone. If you're a "road dog" you don't have much direct supervision, but troopers are continually in contact with their communications centers to check in with superiors and receive orders. You have to be prepared to work outdoors for long periods of time in all kinds of weather. And you will be required to wear—and must be prepared to use—a gun.

While most of your daily duties will be routine—such as clocking the speed of passing vehicles or helping motorists—at some point you're likely to encounter more dramatic situations. Some state troopers have delivered babies, others have stopped people from committing suicide. But sometimes a trooper is not able to save lives. State police officers are among the first to arrive at the scene of a highway accident. At these times, you will have to be the ultimate professional, providing emergency care, gathering evidence on the cause of the accident, and helping others to cope.

HAVE YOU GOT WHAT IT TAKES?

To perform successfully as a state police officer, you need to possess several different kinds of strengths. First, there's physical ability. You have to stay in excellent shape and be ready to handle a variety of situations that require strength, endurance and agility.

Emotional stability and good character are also critical. Anyone in this line of work must clearly have a sense of responsibility and respect for authority. A good state trooper needs to be fair and open-minded, honest, even-tempered, tactful, quick-thinking, disciplined and self-confident. He or she must be able to make decisions independently, cope with high levels of stress, and exercise sound judgment.

State police should enjoy working with people and serving people who come from different backgrounds and have different beliefs—of any race, religion, sex, sexual preference, age or socioeconomic group. They must treat all people equally and fairly under the law.

Important Skills to Develop

In addition, a top-notch trooper possesses a number of other qualities that enhance his or her ability to get the job done well. These include:

- *Good oral and written communication skills.* State police work involves constant communication. Troopers are called on to deal with all kinds of people in all kinds of situations. In the course of a day, you may have to stop a speeding driver, help a distraught motorist stranded on the road, or testify in a court case. In each of these very different situations, you have to be able to express yourself in an appropriate and effective manner. The ability to write clearly and concisely is also important,

since state police officers continually file detailed reports that may become legal evidence in a court case.

- *Good observation skills.* As a state police officer, you will be expected to accurately report on what you see and hear at the scene of an accident or arrest. This includes being able to draw accurate sketches of accident scenes. Your ability to notice and remember telling details can be very important in conducting investigations, writing reports, and testifying in court cases. It's also very useful to be alert in picking up on suspicious behavior.

- *Good driving skills.* Many state police officers spend most of their time on the road, sometimes in hazardous weather conditions or high-speed pursuits. The better your driving skills, the more safely and adeptly you will be able to handle these situations.

THE APPLICATION PROCESS

From what you've read so far, you've got a good sense of what this job's all about. Next comes learning about how the application process works. First off, some of the typical basic requirements include:

- A minimum age, usually between 18 and 21
- Excellent health and good vision and hearing
- U.S. citizenship; most states also have a residency requirement
- A high school diploma or its equivalent; some states have a higher education requirement
- A valid driver's license for the state
- A clean criminal record

Chapter 6 offers more details about how state troopers in your state are selected. But here are a few procedures that are likely:

- A written exam that typically tests such areas as reading comprehension, observation and memory, and communication skills
- A thorough medical exam
- Various tests of physical ability
- A psychological or personality evaluation
- A thorough background investigation
- An oral interview with a panel of state police officers

- In some states, drug testing and a polygraph (lie detector) test

Like other kinds of law enforcement work, state policing is an attractive career option to many people, and the number of qualified candidates often exceeds the number of job openings in some state police departments. In Texas, for example, the Department of Public Safety hadn't done any hiring between 1990 and 1994. So when hiring resumed, the DPS was deluged with 9,000 applications for 130 positions. With competition this tough, it helps to get any kind of edge you can. (See sidebar for suggestions.)

GAINING THAT COMPETITIVE EDGE

Competition for state police jobs is tough, so any special abilities or experiences you offer could be to your advantage in getting accepted as a new recruit. Here are some areas that may prove useful to develop:

- **Education.** All state police departments require at least a high school diploma. But recently, an increasing number of states are asking for at least some college training. In 1993, 4 percent of state police agencies required a four-year college degree, 10 percent wanted a two-year college degree, and 14 percent had a nondegree college requirement. Whatever the requirement in your state, it can't hurt to go beyond it. It would be particularly useful to explore programs in such relevant fields as law enforcement, criminal justice, or political science. Other courses helpful in preparing for a state police career include psychology, counseling, English, American history, public administration, public relations, sociology, law, chemistry and physics.
- **Second Languages.** Whether you are assisting motorists or conducting investigations, knowing more than one language can be very useful. Granted, you can't expect to become an expert in dozens of languages so that you can communicate with any person you meet who doesn't speak English. But you could focus on learning a second language (speaking and/or writing) that is common among citizens in the area where you work.
- **Computer Skills.** In state policing, as in just about every other occupation, computer literacy is becoming critical as electronic communication and record-keeping becomes the norm—not only at headquarters, but from your patrol car as well. That said, take a basic computer skills class (add basic typing lessons if you don't already know your way around a keyboard). Practice by using a library's computer system to do research; accessing a database there is similar to using a police database to run a vehicle or driver background check. Or get yourself a computer and practice at home.

WHEN YOU'VE MADE THE GRADE

When you meet all the requirements of the state police agency to which you're applying, your name is added to a list of eligible candidates. Recruits are chosen from this list as vacancies open up in the ranks. How quickly you make it from the list to the force varies from state to state and can be affected by budgetary considerations.

New recruits undergo extremely rigorous formal training that often lasts several months. The program at the state police academy in New York, for instance, runs for 24 weeks, while the one in California goes 27 weeks. Trooper trainees usually receive instruction in such areas as criminal law and state motor vehicle codes; laws and procedures concerning arrest, search and seizure; traffic control and accident prevention; investigation methods; ethics; communications; community relations; use of firearms; self-defense; high-speed driving; first aid; and handling emergencies. In 1993, the median number of classroom training hours required for new state police officers was 800, while the median number of field training hours was 320.

Once you've successfully completed your training, you'll be assigned to duty, usually working with veteran officers until you learn the ropes. Keep in mind that for your first duty, you could be stationed anywhere in the state, not necessarily in the area in which you currently live. You'll be serving on a probationary basis for a period of anything from six months to a year or more, depending on the state. After that, if your work is satisfactory, your employment becomes permanent.

Moving On—and Up

As you move on in your career, you'll find that many state police departments help troopers to keep up with the latest in law enforcement and improve their job performance by offering ongoing training programs in a variety of areas. These range from super-visory training to seminars in criminal investigative techniques to courses on ethics, human relations and communications.

While many state troopers enjoy being out in the field handling a wide variety of duties, some choose to specialize in a particular function. In many states there may be opportunities in such areas as training new recruits, fingerprint analysis, ballistics testing, and laboratory analysis of criminal evidence.

When it comes to moving up the career ladder, promotions are generally made based on job performance and scoring on a written examination. The ranks you can aspire to include Corporal, Sergeant, First Sergeant, Lieutenant, Captain, Major, Inspector, Deputy Superintendent, and Superintendent. (Titles or rankings may differ by state.) Anyone who meets the qualifications for a higher position can take the promotional exam for it.

> ### JUST THE FACTS
> **The National Uniform Manufacturers Association, which holds a contest each year for best uniform, named the Connecticut State Police as the best-dressed law enforcement officers in the country in 1995.**

ISSUES AND TRENDS

As an aspiring state police officer, you'll want to keep on top of what's going on in the country, and especially your state, that could have an impact on the way troopers do their job. There are a number of "hot" issues and trends in the field of law enforcement and criminal justice that are likely to be commanding attention for some time to come.

Recent opinion polls and election results have indicated loud and clear that the public is saying get tough on crime. Crime is one of the most serious social issues of the day, and people are becoming ever more fearful about the proliferation of drug- and gang-related violence in our communities. So you know that the kind of work state police officers are doing is ever more important in our society.

But at the same time that the public wants stronger law enforcement, many citizens seem to have lost respect for the officers who do the enforcing. Recent high-profile trials, such as those of O.J. Simpson and the officers accused of beating Rodney King, were accompanied by endless commentary about the questionable conduct of some police officers. While these cases didn't involve state troopers, all law enforcement officers have been affected, as many citizens have lost faith in the men and women sworn to protect them. This negative attitude can be very demoralizing for a state police officer who is putting his or her life on the line every day—not to mention possible departmental or legal inquiry if their actions are questioned.

High-Tech Tools for the Next Century

On a more positive note, troopers are getting state-of-the-art tools that are helping them to do their jobs more quickly and efficiently. In particular, state police departments are rapidly pulling onto the information superhighway with the increasing use of computers. In 1993, state police agencies most frequently used computers for such routine functions as record-keeping, fleet management, and budgeting. But a significant number also used them for crime investigation (63 percent) and analysis (45 percent).

And many states are now taking the next high-tech step forward, installing computers in patrol cars. This is a real boon to troopers, making it much easier for them to communicate with each other, conduct immediate vehicle and criminal checks, and perform routine paperwork. The Washington State Patrol, for example, recently equipped many of its cruisers with a 486 notebook computer with a 120-megabyte hard disk drive, modem and two-way radio. So in a few years, it's likely that computer literacy will not just be an advantage for aspiring state troopers, but a necessity.

MAKING THE COMMITMENT

If you're determined to carve out a career for yourself as a state police officer, do yourself a favor and start to prepare *now*, regardless of when the next exam is scheduled. Listed below are some ways to get yourself moving. Many are the same as the tips provided in the previous chapter on police officers. They're worth repeating because the same advice applies to you as a candidate for the state police.

- *Get fit.* Working out regularly and participating in sports will help you develop the strength, stamina and agility needed for state police work. Try enrolling in martial arts classes. Martial arts are valuable not only for their practical techniques of self-defense, but also for their mind/body connection that can help you remain centered and focused under stressful circumstances.
- *Conduct your own background investigation.* Go to the library and go online to read all you can about law enforcement in general and state policing in particular. Many police organizations and government agencies publish newsletters that are available to non-members. The criminal justice departments of colleges and universities are a good source of books, newsletters, academic papers, and research reports. Call the public information office of the state police in the state(s)

you're interested in and see if they have a brochure, annual report or press kit to send you. Read the paper daily to keep up not only on news about state police officers and departments, but also on social issues, legal matters and new laws, crime trends and other areas that directly affect state police work. If you have access to a computer and can get on the Internet, you'll find a wealth of material on law enforcement. (See sidebar for an introductory guide to going online.)

- *Do some networking.* The best way to learn about what it's like to be a state trooper is to talk to people who are on the force. If you don't know anyone, ask family, friends and acquaintances if *they* know someone—word will get around and the chances are that sooner or later you'll be able to identify someone who can answer your questions and give you some pointers. You can also make friends in cyberspace—there are a number of online discussion groups in the law enforcement

area, and at least one dedicated specifically to state troopers (see sidebar).

- *Get ready for the written exam.* In general, the written exam will gauge your skills in such areas as logical reasoning, good judgment, problem-solving, observation and memory for details, basic grammar and writing skills, and reading comprehension. Don't wait until the night before the test to start getting ready. The more you prepare, the more relaxed and confident you'll be when you actually sit down to take the exam.

- *Prepare for the oral interview.* A lot of people become shy and self-conscious talking about their background, skills and ambitions with a stranger. But you're going to have to do that—and convincingly—when you go through the interview that is part of the application process. Thinking about your answers beforehand may help to reduce your anxiety about the interview process. Why do you want to become a state trooper? What are your

RESOURCES IN CYBERSPACE

If you have a computer and access to online services and the Internet, there are plenty of places to find out more about the field of law enforcement. The previous chapter listed several Web sites that are of interest to police and state police officers alike (see the sidebar in Chapter 2, "Surfing the Beat"). In addition, check out another online resource called the State Troopers Forum. America Online (AOL) carries this bulletin board/discussion group, which features lively contributions from state police officers, "wanna-be" troopers, and interested citizens from all over the country. The postings range from fun (a raucous report on a recent regional picnic) to sadly serious (announcements of troopers who have died in the line of duty). This forum is frequented by a lot of people who want to become state troopers, seeking advice on everything from the testing dates and hiring situations in particular states to what to expect on the exams and interviews. The troopers who participate tend to be very proud of their profession and supportive of each other and those interested in joining their ranks. [AOL path: Clubs and Interests/Professional Organizations/Public Safety/1st Precinct/State Troopers Forum] goals on the force? What kind of knowledge, abilities and experiences do you bring to the job? Once you've put your answers into words—even writing them down, if that helps—practice telling them to someone else—a friend or family member, perhaps. The idea is not to have memorized or "canned" responses, but to be clear about your choice, your potential and your talents so you feel comfortable talking about them.

It takes deep dedication and a lot of hard work to become a state police officer. But those who have made it through the arduous application process and the tough training to join the elite world of state troopers think it's worth the effort—to hear them talk, they have the best job in the world. If you think you've got what it takes, give it all you've got.

C · H · A · P · T · E · R
THE WORK OF A CORRECTIONS OFFICER 4

CHAPTER SUMMARY

If you want to know whether a career as a corrections officer suits you, just keep reading. This chapter describes typical duties, the fast-growing job prospects and the nature of the work. You'll find information about the hiring process and tips on making yourself a top-notch candidate. You'll also find plenty of facts about current trends in corrections at the federal, state and local level.

Today's corrections officer is much more than "just a guard." Prisons and other correctional facilities are always on the lookout for applicants who are quick thinkers, able learners, good leaders and physically and emotionally strong.

Those are important traits because it takes a variety of skills and knowledge—not to mention stamina—to do this job. For example, corrections officers are taking on more duties related to counseling and rehabilitating inmates. This requires special training in areas such as understanding criminal behavior, or how to deal with groups of inmates who come from different cultural and ethnic backgrounds, or how to manage the tension that builds among people who are confined to a cell and cut off from the outside world. Technical knowledge also is becoming more important for this job. Where budgets allow, many facilities are putting in high-tech safety and security devices. Corrections officers are the ones who have to be able to operate these sophisticated systems.

There's also a lot to cope with in terms of the working conditions. It's a fact that many prisons are overcrowded and underfunded, that more violent offenders are behind bars than ever before and that drug use among inmates is widespread. These and other major changes have added strain to an already tough environment.

Sheer numbers tell more of the tale: the U.S. prison population has more than tripled since 1980. The Bureau of Justice Statistics (BJS) reported a total of 1,053,738 prisoners under state or federal jurisdiction at the end of 1994. More than 950,000 of those are housed in state facilities and over 95,000 in federal facilities. As for local jails, the inmate population reached a record high of 490,442 as of midyear 1994, partly because they're taking on the overflow when there's no room left in state and federal prisons.

As the number of inmates continues to climb, so does the need for corrections officers. All in all, this is both a demanding job and a job that's in demand.

The Daily Routine

The fundamental responsibility of a corrections officer is to make sure that a prison, jail or other type of correctional facility stays safe and secure. To do this, they guard, supervise and give guidance to criminal offenders who are confined to the facility. They must enforce the rules of the facility, keep things as peaceful as possible and prevent inmates from escaping.

Corrections officers monitor the activities and behavior of inmates at all times—when they're sleeping, showering, eating, working, exercising, etc. They escort inmates to and from cells and other areas of the prison and, as needed, back and forth from outside areas such as courtrooms or medical facilities. They explain the institution's policies and regulations to inmates, and also may schedule the inmates' work assignments and take part in vocational training.

Search and inspection are regular duties. This includes everything from reading inmates' mail to inspecting cells to conducting body searches of inmates. These duties are aimed at finding any forbidden items or materials (such as drugs, weapons, tools or other contraband) or uncovering any criminal activities (such as smuggling operations or plans for escape). Along with admitting and escorting authorized visitors, corrections officers also may monitor conversations between inmates and visitors.

On the Alert

Depending on how a facility is set up and its size, corrections officers may be assigned to specific areas such as the laundry room, mailroom, motor pool, or an on-site medical center. Certain specialized tasks may also be available, such as being part of the road crew or canine unit. Some work assignments involve little or no contact with inmates. For example, corrections officers are stationed at security posts at the prison gates or in towers surrounding the prison, or may guard the facilities using high-tech surveillance and security equipment. Security duties include patrolling the grounds and buildings to make sure that locks, bars and doors are secure. Corrections officers also check medical and food supply areas for possible thefts and are always on the lookout for unsanitary or unsafe conditions, especially fire hazards.

A vital role of corrections officers is to discipline and keep order among inmates. They must watch for signs of tension or conflict in order to prevent physical violence or emergency situations such as riots. At times this can require the use of force or weapons. Delivering first aid or basic medical treatment also may be necessary. However, while corrections officers must

INSTITUTIONAL AND COMMUNITY CORRECTIONS

Nearly 4.9 million persons were under some form of correctional supervision as of the end of 1993, including 2.8 million adults on probation and 671,000 on parole. The following shows the percentage distribution of the total corrections population for that year.

Under confinement	28.0%
Federal prisons	1.7
State prisons	17.0
Local jails	9.3
Under community supervision	72.0%
Parole	13.7
Probation	58.3

(Source: Bureau of Justice Statistics)

enforce the rules of a prison, they also must protect inmates and stay within the boundaries of prisoners' rights.

> JUST THE FACTS:
> **Successful escapes are virtually impossible at the Security Housing Unit of Pelican Bay State Prison in Crescent City, California—the electric fence surrounding this maximum security unit can deliver a shock of 5,100 volts.**

Preparing written reports are another part of the job. These may include keeping daily logbooks and writing conduct or progress reports about inmates. These reports must be accurate and complete because they may be used by parole boards or by the courts. Corrections officers also need to inform their supervisors in person of any fights, suspicious activity or violations of prison rules that may occur.

Of course, what corrections officers do on the job depends to some extent on *where* they're doing their job. Corrections officers work in various places, including federal or state prisons, city or county jails, boot camps, reformatories or detention centers. These facilities come in different sizes and use different levels of security. For example, a maximum security prison may be walled or double-fenced and have gun towers, numerous security devices, cell housing for inmates and a large staff to supervise inmates. A boot camp, on the other hand, may have patrol guards (instead of being fenced or walled), dormitory housing (instead of cells) and a lower staff-to-inmate ratio. Because of these differences, both the duties you'd perform and how much danger you'd face on a daily basis would be affected by the kind of institution you work for.

Setting the Tone

Corrections officers must walk a fine line. They have to be tough disciplinarians to keep inmates in line. Yet they also have to be fair and humane in order to earn the inmates' respect. When it comes right down to it, corrections officers and inmates spend a lot of time together; trying hard to walk that fine line is in everyone's best interest.

If you want to see a movie version of how *not* to improve relations between inmates and officers, just pop "Cool Hand Luke" into your VCR some night. Paul Newman stars as a prisoner (Luke) working on a chain gang. The chief guard and his cronies are determined to break the spirit of Luke and the other prisoners using vicious, strong-arm tactics. Since it's the movies, the cruelty of the guards has to be exaggerated so that Newman's character can wind up the tragic hero. Still, the film does show how power and authority can be abused—how those in charge can go too far to get prisoners to follow the rules. When the chief delivers the classic line "What we have here is a failure to communicate," he's absolutely right.

Good communication skills are, in fact, one of the most important traits you can bring to the job. As a corrections officer, you're not only there to keep the facility secure and make sure no inmates escape. You have a duty to ensure the safety and well-being of prison inmates. Some of the inmates you may be dealing with will never be released. Others will one day be back in society, trying to get on with their lives. You can influence how well they make that transition.

Setting the Example

Part of the influence you can have as a corrections officer has to do with your general attitude about criminals and the way you act toward inmates—basically, how good you are at walking that fine line between being tough and being fair. But there's also a more specific role that involves helping social workers, psychologists, parole and probation officers, teachers and other people who are working to rehabilitate and educate inmates. You'll be a member of that team.

JUST THE FACTS:
Located on a remote island near San Francisco, the U.S. Penitentiary Alcatraz housed 1,545 inmates during its operation from 1934-1963— including a few notorious characters such as Al Capone, George "Machine Gun" Kelly and Robert Franklin Stroud (otherwise known as "the Birdman of Alcatraz"). Though built as an experiment in the extreme isolation of prisoners, Alcatraz closed both for financial reasons and because its isolated conditions didn't fit the then-emerging trend of inmate rehabilitation.

That could mean helping to develop inmates' reading and writing skills; to keep them free from drug and alcohol abuse; to prepare them for employment upon their release; or to sort through personal problems. Your training as a corrections officer will include ways of teaching and counseling inmates. Many prisons offer advanced training in the skills corrections officers need to conduct one-on-one or group counseling sessions.

Your ability to communicate matters in other ways as well. You'll be giving instructions to inmates about prison regulations, explaining their work assignments and supervising them in their daily routine. You'll need to understand prison policies and follow orders yourself. Plus you've got to keep the lines of communication open and clear with other officers and your supervisors. And last but not least, you need to be able to communicate in writing to prepare various kinds of reports.

Jobs on the Rise

The fact that prison populations are soaring higher isn't such good news for society, but it does mean that job prospects are favorable for corrections officers.

According to the U.S. Bureau of Labor Statistics (BLS), job opportunities for corrections officers are expected to rise faster than the average for all other occupations. Literally tens of thousands of job openings are expected every year for at least another decade. Facilities that already exist are being expanded and new facilities are being built, which boosts the need for corrections officers. There's also a trend toward giving longer sentences and reducing parole for criminal offenders, meaning more inmates will be held for longer periods of time and thus more corrections officers will be needed to supervise them. Since this job has high turnover, job openings often come about to replace officers who leave. However, there is a good deal of job security because layoffs are rare—after all, at most places the number of inmates is getting higher, not lower, so corrections officers are usually sorely needed.

> **JUST THE FACTS:**
> The Administrative Maximum Facility ("AdminMax") located in Florence, Colorado is known as "the Alcatraz of the Rockies." Opened in 1994 to the tune of $60 million ($123,571 per bed), this ultra-modern federal facility was built to house 484 high-risk criminals—mostly those brought in from other federal prisons for bad conduct.

The BLS reports that corrections officers held about 282,000 jobs in 1992. Only a few thousand of these worked at federal prisons, while about 60% worked at state facilities, including prisons, prison camps and reformatories. Census figures from the Bureau of Justice Statistics (BJS) showed a total of 117,900 corrections officers working in local jails as of June, 1993 (see sidebar). There are many local jails across the country, though they are generally small and hire few officers. The majority of corrections officers work in larger institutions located in rural areas.

CORRECTIONS IN LOCAL JAILS

- The number of corrections officers working in local jails increased 165% from 1983 to 1993.
- Female staff in local jails almost doubled between 1988 and 1993. Men made up 76% of corrections officers and women 24% by midyear 1993.
- The racial and ethnic background of corrections officers working in local jails in 1993 was 69% white, 23% African American and 7% Hispanic.

(Source: "Jails and Jail Inmates 1993-94: Census of Jails and Survey of Jails," US Department of Justice, Office of Justice Programs, Bureau of Justice Statistics)

The Hours and the Earnings

On average, corrections officers work 8-hour shifts, 5 days a week. Some institutions have other schedules such as 4 days working, then 2 days off. Because correctional facilities require 24-hour protection, every work schedule includes working nights, weekends and holidays. You can expect lots of overtime and some double shifts, plus you may be called in during emergencies. Depending on your assignments, you may be working either indoors or outdoors.

As for the wages you'll earn, this changes depending on the employer. You can figure on a starting salary of around $18,000 to $20,000 at state institutions; and roughly the same or slightly lower at local facilities. Federal corrections officers typically start above $20,000 (partly to reflect the fact that a college education or related work experience is required for new hires by the Federal Bureau of Prisons). Gaining more on-the-job experience and extra education or training can lead to both salary increases and promotions. Corrections officers may be moved up to positions that involve supervising other officers, administrative duties, or counseling. They also may use their experience to move into related areas such as probation and parole.

This job typically offers standard benefit packages, including major medical, hospital, disability and life insurance; paid vacation days, holidays and sick leave; and a retirement plan. Many institutions offer extra benefits such as dental coverage, vision care plans and credit unions. Uniforms and equipment are usually provided by the institution. Educational benefits are becoming more common, such as paying for corrections officers to attend college or special training courses, or offering extra salary for those who take courses or earn degrees on their own. Institutions also may offer various "employee assistance programs" (EAPs), for example, financial or legal aid, stress management classes, substance abuse counseling, and personal or family counseling.

> **JUST THE FACTS:**
> The jail population in twenty-one states more than doubled from 1983 to 1993. Texas alone reported 264% growth in jail inmates in 1993. California, Texas, Florida, New York and Georgia together held just under half of all local jail inmates that same year. (Source: Bureau of Justice Statistics)

The Daily Grind

Going into this job, it's important to be realistic about the working environment. Certain threats and dangers are part of the package. And despite all the talk of "country club" prisons, you'd be hard pressed to find a correctional facility that looked like a resort in Palm Beach.

The most basic fact to consider is that you'll be dealing with convicted criminals. A 1995 report issued by the Bureau of Justice Statistics (BJS) showed that violent offenders accounted for most (42%) of the growth in the state prison population between 1980 and 1993. In federal prisons, the number of violent offenders was second only to drug law violators, who made up the single largest group (60%) of federal inmates in 1993. Based on the latest BJS census and survey of jails, drug law violators also are the largest source of growth among inmates in local jails. In addition, nearly half (45%) of the inmates in state and federal prisons combined have been in prison three or more times before.

These figures tell you something about why most inmates are in prison. Many, though not all, have committed violent or despicable crimes. Among the lot are gang members, rapists, child molesters, murderers, thieves, drug users and drug pushers. Yet as a corrections officer, it is your duty to give fair and decent treatment to every prisoner. You'll also be involved in the rehabilitation of prisoners. So now's the time to ask yourself some tough questions.

For starters, how do you think you'll cope being around these kinds of individuals on a daily basis? Can you handle the built-in level of potential violence? Can you give fair and decent treatment to a prisoner whose attitudes and views are offensive to you? Can you put up with verbal and possibly physical abuse? Can you put aside any of your own prejudices and stereotypes in dealing with inmates whose racial, ethnic, religious or cultural background is different from your own? Can you keep an open mind about the chances of some inmates being able to serve their time and go on to lead law-abiding lives after being released? In effect, can you deal with inmates as individuals, rather than lumping them all together as "the undesirables?"

JUST THE FACTS:

At year-end 1993, almost two-thirds of all state and federal prison inmates were African American, Asian, Native American or Hispanics. African Americans were 7 times more likely than whites to have been incarcerated in state or federal prisons. The incarceration rate for Hispanics (of any race) more than tripled from 1980 to 1993, making them the fastest growing minority group in U.S. prisons. (Source: Bureau of Justice Statistics)

A Test of Your Mettle

Something else to consider is the prospect that you'll be working in overcrowded conditions. According to BJS findings, state correctional facilities were operating on average at least 17% above their intended capacity; federal facilities were 25% over capacity. (The "intended capacity" is the highest number of prisoners a facility

was built to hold.) At the end of 1994, a total of 48,949 state prisoners in 23 jurisdictions were being held in local jails or other facilities due to crowding in state facilities. These are key figures because tension tends to mount in these conditions, which can lead to more violence, more attempts at escape or full-scale riots.

The general atmosphere of the workplace is another matter. Correctional facilities simply aren't pretty places. A lot of the daily duties are tedious, such as doing routine headcounts and paperwork and sitting or standing for long periods of time. A major issue is that prisoners and corrections officers generally don't trust each other much. You'll have to deal with many inmates who are resentful, depressed or openly hostile about being there. In addition, their criminal behavior doesn't always stop just because they're behind bars. For example, violence and sexual abuse among inmates and the smuggling of drugs and weapons are common problems at many prisons.

This leads to another issue: that it's not only the inmates who may behave this way. You might encounter fellow corrections officers who join in smuggling schemes for personal profit. Some officers may take out their own frustration and hostility on the inmates through cruel or violent treatment. For other officers, not being able to cope emotionally may lead to problems at home, substance abuse or a clinical depression. These are not necessarily typical reactions, but they do occur even among the most dedicated and strong of the bunch.

If you're going to do this job well, you need to give some thought in advance to what the workplace is like. Many facilities are active in training and counseling corrections officers to help manage the daily pressures. It also may help to keep in mind that the work of a corrections officer is very important work. Corrections officers are part of a vital system that aims to protect society from harm.

JUST THE FACTS:
In 1994, the local jail population was made up of 39% white non-Hispanics; 44% black non-Hispanics; 15% Hispanics; and 2% non-Hispanics of other races. (Source: Bureau of Justice Statistics)

- Background investigation (felony convictions are generally an automatic disqualifier; misdemeanors may be judged on an individual basis, depending on the nature of the offense)
- Medical exam (including vision and hearing tests and meeting height/weight standards)
- Physical performance tests
- Drug screening and a polygraph (lie detector) test
- Oral interview

Landing the Job

Now you've got the lowdown of what's involved in being a corrections officer: the nature of the work, the job prospects, what you'll earn, the every day duties and the dangers. If you're ready and willing to take on the challenge, the next step is to start applying for the job.

The application and selection process will differ somewhat depending on whether you're applying to federal, state or local institutions. Certain typical standards are listed below. However, one important exception to these is that *federal* prisons require either a four-year college degree or three years of work experience in law enforcement or corrections.

Minimum Requirements

- Minimum age between 18 and 21
- High school diploma or a General Equivalency Diploma(GED)
- Valid driver's license and a good driving record
- U.S. citizenship at time of appointment
- Responsible work history or honorable discharge from military service, if applicable

Procedures

- Written examination measuring areas such as reading comprehension, observation and memory and communication skills
- Psychological testing

Along with the above, some institutions include a residency requirement. Also be aware that some state and local facilities have adopted higher education requirements for entry-level corrections officers. Usually this means a certain number of college credits, not necessarily a degree. In any event, higher education can give you an advantage in the hiring process. Prior military service and related work experience are other advantages. Being fluent in other languages that are common to the inmate population is another plus.

Meeting Your Future

There's a lot of learning you can do right now to help prepare yourself for a career in corrections. One of the best things you can do is to find out about major trends and issues in corrections, law enforcement and the criminal justice system. Once you have a good sense of both the challenges and opportunities involved, you then can explore ways to develop the mindset and skills you'll need to be successful in this career.

The main trend to be aware of goes back to the fact that the prison and jail population has swelled over the past two decades and shows no signs of shrinking in the near future. With over 1 million inmates in prisons and jails, the U.S. now has the highest recorded rate of imprisonment per capita of any country in the world. Meanwhile, the battle against crime continues

KEY PERSONAL TRAITS

- Emotionally mature and stable
- Good communication and interpersonal skills
- Alert, able to think and act quickly
- Good leadership and supervisory skills
- Diplomatic, patient and a good listener
- Reliable and honest
- Ethical and fair
- Accepting of racial, ethnic, cultural and religious differences
- Sympathetic yet realistic understanding of human behavior
- Strong sense of self, not easily manipulated or offended
- Physical strength and stamina

on the streets with more arrests and in the courts with harsher sentencing practices.

At the federal level, a major factor in the growth of the prison population was the "truth in sentencing" guidelines that stemmed from the Sentencing Reform Act of 1984. These guidelines take into account how serious a crime is and the criminal record of the offender when sentences are made. Because this raised the odds of federal offenders being convicted, the number of offenders sent to federal prisons rose in turn—a whopping 144% between 1980 and 1992, according to the latest BJS calculations.

In state prisons, growth in the inmate population resulted mostly from a larger number of adult arrests for serious offenses, leading to more offenders then being put in prison. Like the federal system, the states experienced a huge 142% rise in prison admissions between 1980 and 1993. Current experiments with "Three Strikes and You're Out" and "Life Without Parole" laws stand to raise new admissions even higher if the legislation sticks.

Local jails have also seen more new admissions due to more arrests. Added to that are more felons being sentenced to local jails. Then there's the larger role that local jails now play as the caretakers for state and federal prisoners. Just think about these statistics: the overall inmate population in local jails grew 106% from 1983-1993; but the number of inmates being held by local jails for state and federal authorities grew at twice that rate (212%). According to the BJS, close to two-thirds of these inmates were being held as a direct result of crowding in state and federal prisons.

JUST THE FACTS:
Women inmates made up only 6.1% of all state and federal prisoners nationwide by year-end 1994. However, the number of female inmates grew at a faster rate than the number of male inmates—10.6% versus 8.5%. (Source: Bureau of Justice Statistics)

LOCAL JAIL: STAFF & INMATES

	Census of Jails 1983	Annual Survey of Jails 1993
Number of jails	3,338	3,304
Number of staff	64,560	165,500
Number of inmates per employee	3.5	2.8
Number of inmates	223,551	459,804
Rated capacity of jails	261,556	475,224
Percent of capacity occupied	85%	97%

(Source: "Jails and Jail Inmates 1993-94: Census of Jails and Survey of Jails," US Department of Justice, Office of Justice Programs, Bureau of Justice Statistics Bulletin)

The Ripple Effect

The population boom in prisons and jails influences your future as a corrections officer in several ways. As noted earlier, it increases the need to expand or build new facilities; and because it takes more staff to run these facilities and supervise prisoners, that spells more job opportunities. But budgets are tight. While the government searches and haggles for the dollars it takes to hire more staff and build new or improved facilities, the current conditions often get worse. Whenever extra cots get added to cells and inmates get crammed and tense, you can count on pressures rising for corrections officers. Fighting and rioting have already become more commonplace. Many institutions are also seeing more physical and emotional health problems among inmates that are linked to crowded conditions.

On top of this are overall changes in the nature and character of the prisoners. Many experts in the field agree that modern criminals are, on the whole, a tougher breed. The sharp rise among drug law offenders is one example, not only because these inmates may have a habit to kick but also because that habit doesn't

necessarily stop behind bars. Inmates selling, buying and using drugs are serious problems at many prisons.

Ethnic and racial diversity among inmates can produce another set of problems. It isn't easy to keep the peace when, for example, you're mingling a largely African American or Hispanic group of urban gang members with cliques of skinheads or white supremacists. This example is extreme, but real. In any event, you can expect to see more training of corrections officers to manage inmates who come from different backgrounds and may have strong group ties, for instance, to a street gang or a radical religious organization. More training is also being aimed at handling special issues such as substance abuse or violence between inmates and against officers.

Experts are still debating the best ways to manage the current inmate population. Correctional boot camps for nonviolent offenders are one experiment being tried. These camps focus on rehabilitation, most often through education, job training and substance abuse counseling or treatment. At the same time, some institutions have gone the opposite direction by reinstating chain gangs. Somewhere in the middle of these two approaches is a movement to get rid of recreational equipment, television and other inmate privileges and programs. Those in favor see too much play and not enough punishment; those against say that these privileges can help to reduce tensions and encourage better behavior. Yet another trend involves private companies getting into the business of running prisons and putting inmates to work, which raises the thorny issue of using prison labor for profit.

In one way or another, your future as a corrections officer will be affected by trends like these—everything from higher rates of arrest and imprisonment to different philosophies about how to handle inmates. The next time you're reading the newspaper and come across stories about the prison system or the legal system, just think about the ripple effect: what those stories mean in "real world" terms to the individuals who are guarding the country's jails and prisons. Someday soon that could be you.

Go For It

As the saying goes, now's the time to plan your work and work your plan. It's true that the overall demand for corrections officers is high, but you still need to show that you're the right candidate for the job. In keeping with the tips mentioned at the end of the previous two chapters, here are some ways to get things rolling for a career in corrections:

- Start a physical fitness program. Learn some stress management techniques. If meditation isn't your thing, try the martial arts as a way to train yourself physically and mentally.
- Find out the application requirements and procedures at state, federal or local correctional facilities in your region.
- Prepare yourself for the written examination and other tests and interviews that are part of the selection process.
- Study up on trends in corrections and related fields. Talk to some knowledgeable folks about the job and do some extra reading. You can even use a computer for both networking and gathering information (see the sidebar called "On-line Corrections Connections").
- Look into formal education in corrections. Take a college class or two, or aim yourself toward a full degree.

The idea behind each of these steps is, of course, to give yourself every edge you can in the application and selection process. Corrections departments are in great need of qualified candidates who are motivated to perform the job. Finding out what's involved and getting yourself prepared goes a long way toward demonstrating that you've got what they're looking for.

ON-LINE CORRECTIONS CONNECTIONS

You can find out a lot about corrections and the prison system by connecting by computer to the Internet and the World Wide Web. See the sidebar in Chapter 2 called "Surfing the Beat" for more information about using these resources. A wide range of corrections-related sites are offered by both professional organizations and individuals—including prisoners! And don't forget to join discussion groups or put yourself on an electronic mailing list with others who are working in or interested in the field. Several of these sites are listed below, along with the on-line address ("URL") you'll need to take you there.

Federal Bureau of Prisons—facts and research related to the federal prison system, including an overview of the organization and its regional offices and facilities. [URL: http//www.usdoj.gov/bop/bop.html]

International Association of Correctional Officers (IACO)—home page of this non-profit organization that is dedicated to serving the professional advancement of correctional officers; includes information about becoming a member and/or subscribing to IACO publications. [URL: http//www.acsp.uic.edu/iaco/about.htm]

The Keeper's Voice—on-line version of the quarterly newsletter published by the IACO, which offers articles about issues, trends and people working in the field of corrections. [URL: http//www.acsp.uic.edu/iaco/kv1601tc.htm]

Secure and Community Corrections—a summary report that links to numerous sites specific to the prison system and the field of corrections, including a variety of research and other material with a "real world" view of prison life. [URL: http//orion.alaska.edu/~afdsw/prison.html]

Life in Prison—a guided tour of two Oregon prisons (one medium, one maximum security) using text and photos to describe the facilities, the daily routine and the on-site manufacturing plants in which the inmates work. [http//www.teleport.com/~jailjean/tourpris.shtml]

Cecil Greek's Criminal Justice Page—in addition to on-line resources covering criminal justice, law enforcement and the legal system, with access to many sites are relevant specifically to corrections and the penal system. [URL: http://www.stpt.usf.edu/~greek/cj.html]

To view things from the prisoner's perspective, check out the following sites that are maintained by individual inmates or inmate activist groups. Topics they cover include inmate rights, legal action and general concerns and tales about prison life.

Prison Issues Desk [URL: http//www.igc.apc.org/prisons/]
Prison Legal News [URL: http//weber.u.washington.edu/~lursa/PLN/pln]
Dante's Prison Page/Prison Resources [URL: www.halcyon.com/dante/dpp/links.html]

C·H·A·P·T·E·R 5

THE POLICE OFFICER SUITABILITY TEST

CHAPTER SUMMARY

Wanting to be a police officer is one thing; being suited for it is something else. The following self-quiz can help you decide whether you and this career will make a good match.

T
here is no one "type" of person who becomes a police officer. Cops are as varied as any other group of people in their personalities, experience, and styles. At the same time, there are some attitudes and behaviors that seem to predict success and satisfaction in this profession. They have nothing to do with your intelligence and ability—they simply reflect how you interact with other people and how you choose to approach the world.

These "suitability factors" were pulled from research literature and discussions with police psychologists and screeners across the country. They fall into five groups; each has ten questions spaced throughout this test.

The LearningExpress Police Officer Suitability Test is not a formal psychological test. For one thing, it's not nearly long enough; the MMPI (Minnesota Multiphasic Personality Inventory) test used in most psychological assessments has 11 times more items than you'll find here. For another, it does not focus on your general mental health.

Instead, the test should be viewed as an informal guide—a private tool to help you decide whether being a police officer would suit you, and whether you would enjoy it. It also provides the opportunity for greater self-understanding, which is beneficial no matter what you do for a living.

THE POLICE OFFICER SUITABILITY TEST

DIRECTIONS

You'll need about 20 minutes to answer the 50 questions below. It's a good idea to do them all at one sitting—scoring and interpretation can be done later. For each question, consider how often the attitude or behavior applies to you. You have a choice between Never, Rarely, Sometimes, Often, and Always; put the number for your answer in the space after each question. For example, if the answer is "sometimes," the score for that item is 10; "always" gets a 40, etc. How they add up will be explained later. If you try to outsmart the test or figure out the "right" answers, you won't get an accurate picture at the end. So just be honest.

PLEASE NOTE: Don't read the scoring sections before you answer the questions, or you'll defeat the whole purpose of the exercise!

How often do the following statements sound like you? Choose one answer for each statement.

NEVER	RARELY	SOMETIMES	OFTEN	ALWAYS
0	5	10	20	40

1. I like to know what's expected of me. ____

2. I am willing to admit my mistakes to other people. ____

3. Once I've made a decision, I stop thinking about it. ____

4. I can shrug off my fears about getting physically hurt. ____

5. I like to know what to expect. ____

6. It takes a lot to get me really angry. ____

7. My first impressions of people tend to be accurate. ____

8. I am aware of my stress level. ____

9. I like to tell other people what to do. ____

10. I enjoy working with others. ____

11. I trust my instincts. ____

12. I enjoy being teased. ____

13. I will spend as much time as it takes to settle a disagreement. ____

14. I feel comfortable in new social situations. ____

15. When I disagree with people, I let them know about it. ____

16. I'm in a good mood. ____

17. I'm comfortable making quick decisions when necessary. ____

18. Rules must be obeyed, even if you don't agree with them. ____

19. I like to say exactly what I mean. ____

20. I enjoy being with people. ____

21. I stay away from doing exciting things that I know are dangerous. _____

22. I don't mind when a boss tells me what to do._____

23. I enjoy solving puzzles. _____

24. The people I know consult me about their problems. _____

25. I am comfortable making my own decisions. _____

26. People know where I stand on things. _____

27. When I get stressed, I know how to make myself relax. _____

28. I have confidence in my own judgment. _____

29. I make my friends laugh. _____

30. When I make a promise, I keep it. _____

31. When I'm in a group, I tend to be the leader. _____

32. I can deal with sudden changes in my routine. _____

33. When I get into a fight, I can stop myself from losing control. _____

34. I am open to new facts that might change my mind. _____

35. I understand why I do the things I do. _____

36. I'm good at calming people down. _____

37. I can tell how people are feeling even when they don't say anything. _____

38. I take criticism without getting upset. _____

39. People follow my advice. _____

40. I pay attention to people's body language. _____

41. It's important for me to make a good impression. _____

42. I remember to show up on time. _____

43. When I meet new people, I try to understand them. _____

44. I avoid doing things on impulse. _____

45. Being respected is important to me. _____

46. People see me as a calm person. _____

47. It's more important for me to do a good job than to get praised for it. _____

48. I make my decisions based on common sense. _____

49. I prefer to keep my feelings to myself when I'm with strangers. _____

50. I take responsibility for my own actions rather than blame others. _____

SCORING

Attitudes and behaviors can't be measured in units, like distance or weight. Besides, psychological categories tend to overlap. As a result, the numbers and dividing lines between score ranges are approximate, and numbers may vary about 20 points either way. If your score doesn't fall in the optimal range, it doesn't mean a "failure"—only an area that needs focus.

It may help to share your test results with some of the people who are close to you. Very often, there are differences between how we see ourselves and how we actually come across to others.

GROUP 1 – RISK

Add up scores for questions 4, 6, 12, 15, 21, 27, 33, 38, 44, and 46

TOTAL = _____

This group evaluates your tendency to be assertive and take risks. The ideal is in the middle, somewhere between timid and reckless: you should be willing to take risks, but not seek them out just for excitement. Being nervous, impulsive, and afraid of physical injury are all undesirable traits for a police officer. This group also reflects how well you take teasing and criticism, both of which you may encounter every day. And as you can imagine, it's also important for someone who carries a gun not to have a short fuse.

- A score between 360 and 400 is rather extreme, suggesting a kind of macho approach that could be dangerous in the field.
- If you score between 170 and 360, you are on the right track.
- If you score between 80 and 170, you may want to think about how comfortable you are with the idea of confrontation.

- A score between 0 and 80 indicates that the more dangerous and stressful aspects of the job might be difficult for you.

GROUP 2 – CORE

Add up scores for questions 2, 8, 16, 19, 26, 30, 35, 42, 47, and 50

TOTAL = _____

This group reflects such basic traits as stability, reliability, and self-awareness. Can your fellow officers count on you to back them up and do your part? Are you secure enough to do your job without needing praise? Because, in the words of one police psychologist, "If you're hungry for praise, you will starve to death." The public will not always appreciate your efforts, and your supervisors and colleagues may be too busy or preoccupied to pat you on the back.

It is crucial to be able to admit your mistakes and take responsibility for your actions, to be confident without being arrogant or conceited, and to be straightforward and direct in your communication. In a job where lives are at stake, the facts must be clear. Mood is also very important. While we all have good and bad days, someone who is depressed much of the time is not encouraged to pursue police work; depression affects one's judgment, energy level, and the ability to respond and communicate.

- If you score between 180 and 360, you're in the ballpark. 360+ may be unrealistic.
- A score of 100-180 indicates you should look at the questions again and evaluate your style of social interaction.
- Scores between 0 and 100 suggest you may not be ready for this job—yet.

GROUP 3 – JUDGMENT

Add scores for questions 3, 7, 11, 17, 23, 28, 37, 40, 43, and 48

TOTAL = _____

This group taps how you make decisions. Successful police officers are sensitive to unspoken messages, can detect and respond to other people's feelings, and make fair and accurate assessments of a situation, rather than being influenced by their own personal biases and needs. Once the decision to act is made, second-guessing can be dangerous. Police officers must make their best judgments in line with accepted practices, and then act upon these judgments without hesitancy or self-doubt. Finally, it's important to know and accept that you cannot change the world single-handedly. People who seek this career because they want to make a dramatic individual difference in human suffering are likely to be frustrated and disappointed.

- A score over 360 indicates you may be trying too hard.
- If you scored between 170 and 360, your style of making decisions, especially about people, fits with the desired police officer profile.
- Scores between 80 and 170 suggest that you think about how you make judgments and how much confidence you have in them.
- If you scored between 0 and 80, making judgments may be a problem area for you.

GROUP 4 – AUTHORITY

Add scores for questions 1, 10, 13, 18, 22, 25, 32, 34, 39, and 45

TOTAL = _____

This group contains the essential attributes of respect for rules and authority—including the "personal authority" of self-reliance and leadership—and the ability to resolve conflict and work with a team. Once again, a good balance is the key. Police officers must accept and communicate the value of structure and control without being rigid. And even though most decisions are made independently in the field, the authority of the supervisor and the law must be obeyed at all times. Anyone on a personal mission for justice or vengeance will not make a good police officer and is unlikely to make it through the screening process.

- A score between 160 and 360 indicates you have the desired attitude toward authority—both your own and that of your superior officers. Any higher is a bit extreme.
- If you scored between 100 and 160, you might think about whether a demanding leadership role is something you want every day.
- With scores between 0 and 100, ask yourself whether the required combination of structure and independence would be comfortable for you.

GROUP 5 – STYLE

Add up scores for questions 5, 9, 14, 20, 24, 29, 32, 36, 41, and 49

TOTAL = _____

This is the personal style dimension, which describes how you come across to others. Moderation rules here as well: police officers should be seen as strong and capable, but not dramatic or heavy-handed; friendly, but not overly concerned with whether they are liked; patient, but not to the point of losing control of a situation. A good sense of humor is essential, not only in the field but among one's fellow officers. Flexibility is another valuable trait—especially given all the changes that can happen in one shift—but too much flexibility can be perceived as weakness.

- A score between 160 and 360 is optimal. Over 360 is trying too hard.
- Scores between 80 and 160 suggest that you compare your style with the above description and consider whether anything needs to be modified.
- If you scored between 0 and 80, you might think about the way you interact with others and whether you'd be happy in a job where people are the main focus.

SUMMARY

The Police Officer Suitability Test reflects the fact that being a successful police officer requires moderation rather than extremes. Attitudes that are desirable in reasonable amounts can become a real problem if they are too strong. For example, independence is a necessary trait, but too much of it creates a "Dirty Harry" type who takes the law into his or her own hands. Going outside accepted police procedure is a bad idea; worse, it can put other people's lives in jeopardy.

As one recruiter said, the ideal police officer is "low key and low maintenance." In fact, there's only one thing you can't have too much of, and that's common sense. With everything else, balance is the key. Keep this in mind as you look at your scores.

This test was developed by Judith Schlesinger, Ph.D., a writer and psychologist whose background includes years of working with police officers in psychiatric crisis interventions.

C · H · A · P · T · E · R 6

HOW LAW ENFORCEMENT OFFICERS ARE SELECTED

CHAPTER SUMMARY

Now that you have a better idea of what various law enforcement positions are really like, you need to know what you'll face if you apply for a job. This chapter walks you through the whole law enforcement recruitment process, from the exam announcement to getting the job.

In order to become a law enforcement officer, you have to go through a selection process that takes from several months to a year or more. Why such a long and complicated process? Because law enforcement work—as a police officer, state trooper or corrections officer—is tough. Whether you're patrolling a beat, the highways or a cell block, you need a lot of positive character traits and varied skills, and the agency you want to work for needs to know that you're qualified.

In most areas, many more people apply for law enforcement positions than can ever be accepted. A large percentage of people who apply fail one or another part of the selection process: the written exam, the physical agility test, the background investigation, the oral interview or board, or the medical or psychological exam. You don't want to be one of those people.

That's one reason you're reading this book: it will tell you what to expect, so you'll know what the typical steps are in becoming an officer. Knowing those steps, you'll have an edge over applicants coming in cold.

Knowing those steps, you can make a realistic assessment of your personality, your background and your skills.

During this assessment, you might find things that make becoming a law enforcement officer unrealistic for you. However, you might instead find weaknesses that *you can correct*—and you can address them *now*, before you get involved in the selection process.

THE ELIGIBILITY LIST

Most law enforcement agencies establish a list of eligible candidates; many such lists rank candidates from highest to lowest. How ranks are determined varies from place to place; sometimes the rank is based solely on the written exam score, sometimes on the oral board, and sometimes on a combination of factors. The point is, even if you make it through the entire selection process, the likelihood that you will be hired as a law enforcement officer often depends on *the quality of your performance* in one or more parts of the selection process.

Make a commitment now: you need to work hard, in advance, to do well on the written exam, the physical agility test, and the oral interview, so that your name will stand out at the top of your agency's eligibility list.

First, though, you need information. You need to know about the selection process for law enforcement officers. This chapter outlines the basic process in its many steps. Most police departments—municipal or state—use all of these steps, though the order may vary and some departments put more or less emphasis on the various steps. Some corrections departments omit one or more of the steps outlined below.

BASIC QUALIFICATIONS

The basic qualifications you need in order to even think about becoming a law enforcement officer vary from agency to agency, city to city, state to state. It's worthwhile to find out what those qualifications are in the agency you want to serve. Some qualifications are pretty standard:

- A minimum age—sometimes 18, more often 20 or 21. Some agencies also have a maximum age, which can range from 30 to 45.
- U.S. citizenship or, in a few places, resident alien status
- A high school diploma or its equivalent and, increasingly, some college or even a college degree
- A clean criminal record
- Excellent physical and mental health, including good vision and hearing and an appropriate weight-to-height ratio
- For state or municipal police, a valid driver's license and a satisfactory driving record

Many jurisdictions, but not all, require that you live in the jurisdiction or nearby. Most agencies, particularly police departments, give preference to otherwise qualified veterans over civilians. This may take the form of a policy, sometimes called a "Veteran's Preference" policy, whereby points are automatically added to the written exam. Is this unfair? No. Military personnel have learned the discipline and many of the skills—such as use of firearms—that are vital to law enforcement work. Veterans are simply better qualified than most other people. Also, for older applicants, some departments subtract the number of years served in the military from an applicant's age to satisfy the upper age requirement.

Automatic Disqualifiers

There are lots of things that can disqualify you, the most important being any trouble with the law in the past. Convicted felons are not welcome as police officers in any jurisdiction, no matter how much they might have reformed their lives since their conviction. In a few places, people whose criminal convictions are far enough in the past can be considered as corrections officers, but such applicants have to compete with a great many people who *don't* have criminal records. Misdemeanors and even traffic tickets can disqualify applicants to some municipal and state police departments. People who use illegal drugs or abuse legal ones need not apply. A dishonorable discharge from the military is also likely to disqualify you. See the section on The Personal History Statement and Background Investigation later in this chapter.

Law enforcement officers have to be in tip-top physical and emotional shape. Disabilities that would not be a problem in other occupations can become disqualifying conditions for law enforcement officers. These disabilities do not have to be obvious or serious ones. For instance, many agencies require perfect color vision, so that a simple and common condition like blue-green color blindness can disqualify an applicant. So can being overweight. See the section on The Medical Exam later in this chapter for more information on applicants with disabilities.

The specific qualifications you need to apply for a given position are usually listed in the exam announcement.

THE EXAM ANNOUNCEMENT

Applying to be a law enforcement officer differs from applying for most other jobs. The differences begin with the exam announcement. You won't see openings in the police department or the state prison advertised in the Help Wanteds. Instead, the city, county or state starts looking for potential officers by means of a special announcement. This announcement will outline the basic qualifications for the position as well as the steps you will have to go through in the selection process. It often tells you some of the duties you will be expected to perform. It may give the date and place of the written exam, which is usually the first step in the selection process.

Get a copy of this announcement. Often your public library will have a copy. Or you can get one directly from the agency or the city, county or state personnel department. (Corrections officer announcements often can be gotten from the prison you're applying to.) If exams are held irregularly, the agency or personnel department may maintain a mailing list, so that you can receive an exam announcement the next time an exam is scheduled. If exams are held frequently, you will sometimes be told to simply show up at the exam site on a given day of the week or month. In those cases you usually get more information about the job and the selection process if you pass the written exam. *Study the exam announcement,* as well as any other material, such as brochures, that the department sends you. You need to be prepared for the whole selection process in order to be successful.

THE APPLICATION

Often the first step in the process of becoming law enforcement officer is filling out an application. Sometimes this is a real application, asking about your education, employment experience, personal data and so on. In this case, the application is really the personal history statement you'll read about below. Anyone whose application shows that they don't meet the basic qualifications will not be invited to participate in the selection process. Sometimes there's just an application to take the written test, with the full application form coming later for those who pass.

When you call for an exam announcement or application, the person who answers the phone may conduct a brief prescreening to make sure that you meet the basic qualifications as to age, education and so on. Answer briefly and politely, and don't launch into your life story. The person on the other end of the line may remember you when it comes time to select names from the eligibility list.

THE WRITTEN EXAM

In most jurisdictions, taking a written exam is the next step in the application process, though in some cases a background interview comes first. (By putting the background interview first, agencies save themselves the expense of testing applicants who don't meet the basic qualifications.)

The written exam is your first opportunity to show that you have what it takes to be a law enforcement officer. As such, it's extremely important. People who don't pass the written exam don't go any farther in the

selection process. Furthermore, the written exam score often figures into applicants' rank on the eligibility list; in some cases, this score by itself determines your rank, while in others it is combined with other scores, such as physical agility or oral interview scores. In those places, a person who merely passes the exam with a score of, say, 70, is unlikely to be hired when there are plenty of applicants with scores in the 90s. The exam bulletin usually specifies what the rank will be based on. (Eligibility lists apply more to police officers and state police than to corrections officers.)

WHAT THE WRITTEN EXAM IS LIKE

Most written exams simply test basic skills and aptitudes: how well you understand what you read, your writing ability, your ability to follow directions, your judgment and reasoning skills, and sometimes your memory or your math. In this preliminary written exam, *you will not be tested on your knowledge of law enforcement policies and procedures, the law, or any other specific body of knowledge.* This test is designed *only* to see if you can read, write, reason and do basic math.

In a few places, taking the exam involves studying written materials in advance and then answering questions about them on the exam. Some of these written materials have to do with the law and police or

---

APPLICATION TIPS

- Neatness and accuracy count. Filling in your apartment number in the blank labeled "city" reflects poorly on your ability to follow directions.
- Most agencies *don't want your resume.* It goes straight into the circular file. Save your time and energy for filling out the application form the agency gives you.
- If you're mailing your application, take care to submit it to the proper address. It might go to the personnel department rather than to the police or corrections department. Follow the directions on the exam announcement.

corrections procedures—but all you have to do is study the guide you're given. You're still being tested just on your reading skills and memory, and there are good reasons for this.

Law enforcement officers have to be able to read, understand and act on complex written materials such as laws, policy handbooks, and regulations. They have to write incident reports and other materials that have to be clear and correct enough to stand up in court or a probation hearing. They have to be able to think independently, because officers get little direct supervision and don't have time to consult with superiors when violence is brewing. They have to be able to do enough math to add up the value of confiscated goods or compute the street price of a drug sold to a dealer for *x* amount per kilo. The basic skills the written exam tests for are skills law enforcement officers use every day.

Most exams are multiple-choice tests of the sort you've often encountered in school. You get an exam book and an answer sheet where you have to fill in little circles (bubbles) or squares with a number 2 pencil. A few agencies, particularly municipal police departments, will also have you write an essay or a mock police report.

Reading Comprehension Questions

Reading comprehension is a part of almost every written law enforcement exam. These reading questions are like the ones you've probably come across in school tests: you're given a paragraph or two to read and then asked questions about it. Questions typically ask you about:

- the main idea of the passage as a whole
- specific facts or details contained in the passage
- the meaning of words or phrases as they are used in the passage
- inferences and conclusions you can draw from what is stated in the passage

Grammar Questions

When the exam announcement says the exam tests writing skills, you're probably facing multiple-choice questions on grammar, spelling and/or vocabulary. Usually a grammar question asks you to choose which of four versions of a sentence is most correct. The incorrect choices might contain:

- incomplete sentences (fragments)
- two or more sentences put together as if they were one (run-ons)
- verbs that don't go with their subjects (*he think*) or that use the wrong tense (*yesterday she goes*)
- pronouns that don't match the noun they refer to (*a person . . . they*)
- other such errors

Sometimes grammar questions also test punctuation or capitalization, usually by giving you a sentence with punctuation marks or capital letters underlined and asking you to choose which one is wrong.

Spelling Questions

Spelling questions might give you a sentence with a word missing and then ask you which of the choices is the correct spelling of the missing word. Or you might be given several different words and asked which one is spelled wrong.

Vocabulary Questions

Vocabulary questions usually ask you to find a *synonym*—a word that means the same—or the *antonym*—a word that means the opposite—of a given word. If you're lucky, that word will come in a sentence that will help you guess its meaning. If you're less lucky, you'll just be given the word and have to choose a synonym or antonym without any help from context.

Another way vocabulary is tested is to give you a sentence with a blank in it and ask you to choose the word that fits best in the sentence.

Math Questions

Math is usually a minor part of a law enforcement exam, if it's included at all. The questions usually test basic arithmetic: just adding, subtracting, multiplying, and dividing whole numbers. Most often the math questions are word problems that present everyday situations: the total value of stolen property, the number of cupcakes you need to give three to all the officers and two to all the civilians in the department, that kind of thing.

A few tests might ask you to work with fractions, decimals, or percentages, but still in real-life situations: how much is left after one person eats half and another person eats a third; the amount of mileage on a car gauge after a certain number of trips; how much you have to pay for a uniform at a 15% discount; and so on.

Memory Questions

Officers have to be able to remember lots of details about things they see and things they read, so observation and memory questions are often a part of law enforcement exams. You may be given a study booklet in advance of the exam and have to answer questions about it during the exam without referring to the book. Or you might be given a picture to look at or a passage to read right there at the exam and then have to answer questions about it, usually without referring to the picture or passage. You may even be shown a videotape and then asked questions about it later.

Judgment Questions

Obviously law enforcement officers need to have good judgment, so some exams include multiple-choice questions designed to test your good judgment and common sense. You may be given laws or procedures and asked to apply them to a hypothetical situation, or you may be asked which hypothetical situation is most likely to indicate dangerous or criminal activity. Answering these questions requires both common sense and an ability to read carefully.

HOW TO PREPARE FOR THE WRITTEN EXAM

Pay close attention to any material the recruiting unit or personnel department puts out about the exam. If there's a study guide, study it. Pay close attention to what you're going to be tested on, and then find similar materials to practice with.

There are lots of books out there with practice test materials in them. Any test prep book that has basic skills questions in it, including reading comprehension, writing and math, will help. For focused, specific preparation, based on police, state police or corrections exams actually given in your state, consider the LearningExpress *Complete Preparation Guides* (order information at the back of this book).

FINDING OUT HOW YOU DID

Applicants are generally notified in writing about their performance on the exam. The notification may simply say whether or not you passed, but it may tell you what your score was. It may also say when you should show up for the next step in the process, which is often a physical agility test.

THE PHYSICAL AGILITY TEST

The physical agility test is the next step in the process for most police departments; some corrections departments omit this step. (You will, however, have to take a medical exam, so being in shape is a must.) If you have

WRITTEN EXAM TIPS

- Ask for and *use* any material the recruiting unit or personnel department puts out about the written test. Some agencies have study guides; some even conduct study sessions. Why let others get a vital advantage while you don't?
- Practice, practice, practice. And then practice some more.
- Try to find some people who have taken the exam recently, and ask them about what was on the exam. Their hindsight—"I wish I had . . ."—can be your foresight.

to take a physical test, you may have to bring a note from your doctor saying that you are in good enough shape to undertake this test before you will be allowed to participate. A few agencies give the medical exam before the physical agility test. They all want to make sure that no one has a heart attack in the middle of the test. This is a clue: Expect the test to be tough.

Law enforcement is, after all, physically demanding work. Not to discourage you, but the physical agility test for police officers and state troopers in some cases is simply designed to find out whether you're in good enough shape to do well in the physical training at the academy. It's the academy that whips recruits into the physical shape officers need to have.

WHAT THE PHYSICAL AGILITY TEST IS LIKE

The exact events that make up the physical agility test vary from place to place, but there's usually a fair amount of running, some lifting or other upper-body strength requirements and often a test of hand strength, which helps to determine whether you'll be able to handle a gun. Some places use calisthenics like sit-ups and push-ups to assess your physical strength; others have an obstacle course. You can find out just what will be required by your agency from the exam announcement or related materials.

HOW TO PREPARE FOR THE PHYSICAL AGILITY TEST

The physical agility test is one area where advance preparation is almost guaranteed to pay off. No matter how good a shape you're in, start an exercise program *now*. You can design your program around the requirements listed in the exam announcement if you want, but any exercise that will increase your stamina, flexibility and strength will help.

If you're *not* in great shape, consult a doctor before you begin. Start slow and easy and increase your activity as you go. And remember that you don't have to do all this work alone. Taking an aerobics class or playing football will help increase your stamina, and you can supplement such activities with ones that work on your strength.

THE PERSONAL HISTORY STATEMENT AND BACKGROUND INVESTIGATION

Either at the beginning of the whole process or after the first couple of cuts are made, the hiring agency will have you fill out a long form about your personal history. You will usually be interviewed about this material by someone from the recruiting unit or personnel department. As the department begins to get serious about considering you, it will conduct an investigation into your

PHYSICAL AGILITY TIPS

Start exercising *now*. Yes, today. Work up to a 45-minute workout at least 4 times a week. If you smoke, stop. If you're overweight, diet along with your exercise. (No one said becoming a law enforcement officer would be easy.)

background, using your application form or personal history statement as a starting point.

This step is probably the most important in the whole process, even though the results may not be reflected in your rank on the eligibility list. This is where the hiring agency checks not only your experience and education, but also, and perhaps more importantly, your character. Do you have the integrity, the honesty, the commitment, the personal stamina, the respect for authority and the law that a law enforcement officer must have? Police and corrections departments go to a lot of trouble and expense to find out.

WHAT THE PERSONAL HISTORY STATEMENT IS LIKE

You take part in the investigation by filling out the personal history form and talking with the interviewer. The form will be long—up to 30 pages—and requires your serious attention and effort. (Corrections officer candidates will face a less extensive but no less important application form.) Assume that everything you say will be double-checked by a trained, experienced investigator. You'll be asked where you were born, where you lived, where you went to school—including elementary school—what you've studied, where you've worked and what you did there, what organizations you have belonged to and on and on. Your whole life will be laid out on paper. You'll have to supply names of teachers, employers, neighbors and relatives, as well as the names of several additional people who can attest to your character and fitness to be an officer.

How to Fill Out the Personal History Statement

Fill the form out completely, looking up dates and places rather than relying on your memory. Attach all documents, such as diplomas or transcripts, you're asked for. Neatness and accuracy count, but one thing counts even more: honesty.

Be completely honest in everything you write and everything you say to the interviewer. Covering up something in your past, even by just not mentioning it, will in itself be taken as evidence that you don't have the integrity it takes to be a police or corrections officer. Yes, past drug use, hospitalizations, scrapes with the law, family or financial difficulties and such can hurt your chances, but not as much as not mentioning them and having them surface during the investigation. Better to acknowledge up front anything that might cause doubt about your fitness to be an officer and deal with it. Convince the interviewer that, though you know you had difficulties in the past, you have since dealt with them and they will not affect your performance now or in the future. The interviewer may have suggestions about how to resolve past "blots" on your record.

WHAT THE BACKGROUND INVESTIGATION IS LIKE

Starting from your personal history statement, a background investigator from the hiring agency will check you out. The investigator will verify what you've said about yourself: Do you in fact have a high school diploma, an honorable discharge, five years' employment with the same firm?

And *then* the investigator will start asking the *real* questions. Your former teachers, landlords, employers, friends and others will be asked by the investigator how long and how well they knew you and what kind of person they found you to be. Did you meet your obligations? How did you deal with problems? Do they know of anything that might affect your fitness to be a police or corrections officer? Your references will lead the investigator to other people who knew you, and when the investigator is finished, he or she will have a pretty complete picture of what kind of person you are.

HOW TO PREPARE FOR THE PERSONAL HISTORY STATEMENT AND BACKGROUND INVESTIGATION

As a candidate for a law enforcement position, the most important way you can improve your performance on the personal history statement is by improving your personal history. You can't change the past, exactly, but you can use the present to improve your chances in the future. You can address problems that might give a background investigator pause: pay your child support and your old traffic tickets, document your full recovery from a serious illness or your drug-free status since high school. You can also take steps to make yourself a more attractive candidate by getting related experience. You can, for instance, do police work as a volunteer, an intern or a paid cadet, or work with a community agency that helps ex-offenders.

THE LIE DETECTOR TEST

Some jurisdictions require a polygraph, or lie detector, test as part of the background investigation process, though the polygraph, if required, is typically one of the last steps you will go through.

There really is no such thing as a lie detector. What the polygraph detects are changes in heart and respiratory rates, blood pressure and galvanic skin resistance (basically a measure of how much you're perspiring). A cuff like the one your doctor uses to take your blood pressure will be wrapped around your arm. Rubber tubes around your trunk will measure your breathing, and clips on your fingers or palm will measure skin response. The theory is that people who are consciously lying get nervous, and their involuntary bodily responses give them away.

Don't worry about being betrayed by being nervous in the first place. Everyone's a little nervous when confronting a new technology. The polygraph examiner will explain the whole process to you. More important, the examiner will ask you a series of questions to establish a baseline both for when you're telling the truth and for when you're not. For instance, the examiner might tell you to answer "No" to every question and then ask you whether your name is George (if it isn't) and whether you drove to the examination today (if you did).

All questions for a polygraph exam have to be in yes-or-no form. You should be told in advance what every question will be. Some questions will be easy lobs like whether you're wearing sneakers. The questions that really count will be ones that relate to your fitness to be a law enforcement officer: whether you've committed a crime, whether you have received speeding tickets, whether you've been arrested. You will probably have been over any problematic areas with the background investigator or other interviewers before, so just tell the truth and try to relax.

PERSONAL HISTORY TIPS

Just one: be honest.

ORAL INTERVIEWS AND BOARDS

The selection process in your chosen jurisdiction may include one or more oral interviews, none of which will be much like other job interviews you've had in the past. There may be an interview connected with your personal history statement, where the interviewer simply tries to confirm or clarify what you've written. An interview is usually part of the psychological evaluation (see below). Most agencies also conduct an oral interview or board that continues the process of determining whether candidates will make good officers.

WHAT THE ORAL BOARD IS LIKE

The oral board for police officers and state troopers typically assesses such qualities as interpersonal skills, communication skills, judgment and decision-making abilities, respect for diversity, and adaptability. The board itself consists of two to five people, who may be sworn officers or civilians. There's usually some variety in the makeup of the board: sworn officers of various ranks and/or civilians from the personnel department or from the community.

The way the interview is conducted depends on the practices of the individual department. You may be asked a few questions similar to those you would be asked at a normal employment interview: Why do you want to be an officer? Why in this department? What qualities do you have that would make you a good officer? You may be asked questions about your personal history. Have answers prepared for such questions in case they come.

Instead of or in addition to such questions, you may be presented with hypothetical situations that you will be asked to respond to. A board member may simply tell you what the situation is and ask you what you would do, or one or more board members may role play the situation, putting you in the place of the officer in charge. You may even see a video that the board members will ask you about after you've seen it.

Increasingly, cities and states have standardized the oral board questions. The same questions are asked of every candidate, and when the interview is over the board rates each candidate on a standard scale. This procedure helps the interviewers reach a somewhat more objective conclusion about the candidates they have interviewed and may result in a score that is included in the factors used to generate the eligibility list. Indeed, some departments have decided that the oral board is so important that this score by itself determines candidates' rank on the list.

HOW TO PREPARE FOR THE ORAL BOARD

If the agency you're applying to puts out any material about the oral board, study it carefully. It will tell you what the board is looking for. It might even give you some sample questions you can practice with.

Think about your answers to questions you might be asked. You might even try to write your own oral board questions and situations. Write down your answers if you want. Practice saying them in front of a mirror until you feel comfortable, but don't memorize them. You don't want to sound like you're reciting from a book. Your answers should sound conversational even though you've prepared in advance.

Then enlist friends or family to serve as a mock oral board. If you know a speech teacher, get him or her to help. Give them your questions, tell them about what you've learned, and then have a practice oral board. Start from the moment you walk into the room. Go through the entire session as if it were the real thing, and then ask your mock board for their feedback on your performance.

It may even help to videotape your mock board session. The camera can reveal things about your body language or habits that you don't even know about.

THE PSYCHOLOGICAL EVALUATION

Before you get offended at having to go through a battery of psychological tests, consider: Do you want the officer backing you up in a tense situation to be a nut case with a gun?

Neither does the agency that's hiring. OK, you're not a nut case, and neither are most of the people applying with you. But remember, law enforcement work is one of the most stressful occupations there is. While no one can guarantee that a given individual won't "crack" under the stress, law enforcement agencies want to weed

out as many people with underlying instabilities as they can, in hopes that those remaining will be able to deal with the problems in healthy ways. Sometimes, too, the real purpose of the psychological evaluation is not so much to disclose instabilities as to determine applicants' honesty, habits and other such factors. Thus, many agencies conduct written or oral psychological evaluations or both.

WHAT THE WRITTEN PSYCHO-LOGICAL EVALUATION IS LIKE

More often than not, the psychological evaluation begins with one or more written tests. These are typically standard tests licensed from a psychological testing company; they are often multiple-choice or true-false tests. The Minnesota Multiphasic Personality Inventory (MMPI) is one commonly used test. The tests may take one hour or several; the hiring agency will let you know approximately how much time to allot.

There's only one piece of advice we can offer you for dealing with a written psychological evaluation: *Don't try to psych out the test.* The people who wrote these tests know more about psyching out tests than you do. They designed the test so that one answer checks against another to find out whether test-takers are lying. Just answer honestly, and don't worry about whether your answers to some of the questions seem

ORAL BOARD TIPS

- Dress neatly and conservatively, as you would for a business interview.
- Be polite; say "please" and "thank you," "sir" or "ma'am."
- Remember, one-half of communication is listening. Look at board members as they speak to you, and listen carefully to what they say.
- Think before you speak. Nod or say "OK" to indicate that you understand the question, and then pause a moment to collect your thoughts before speaking.
- If you start to feel nervous, take a deep breath, relax and just do your best.

to you to indicate that you might be nuts after all. They probably don't.

WHAT THE ORAL PSYCHOLOGICAL EVALUATION IS LIKE

Whether or not there is a written psychological examination, there is usually an oral interview with a psychologist or psychiatrist, who may be either on the hiring agency's staff or an independent contractor. The psychologist may ask you questions about your schooling and jobs, your relationships with family and friends, your habits, your hobbies. Since there's such a broad range of things you could be asked about, there's really no way to prepare. In fact, the psychologist may be more interested in the way you answer—whether you come across as open, forthright, and honest—than in the answers themselves.

Once again, honesty is the best policy; there's no point in playing psychological games with someone who's better trained at it than you are. Try to relax, and answer openly. The psychologist is not trying to trick you and isn't really interested in your feelings about your mother unless they're so extreme that they're going to make you unfit to be an officer.

THE MEDICAL EXAMINATION

Before passage of the Americans With Disabilities Act (ADA), many law enforcement agencies conducted a medical examination early in the process, before the physical agility test. Now, the ADA says it's illegal to do any examinations or ask any questions that could reveal an applicant's disability until after a conditional offer of employment has been made. That means that in most jurisdictions you will get such a conditional offer before you are asked to submit to a medical exam. Indeed, you may get such an offer before the polygraph examination, the psychological examination, or, in a few cases, even before the background investigation, precisely because all these components could reveal a disability.

Drug Testing

Note, however, that a test for use of illegal drugs *can* be administered before a conditional offer of employment, and most law enforcement agencies use this option. If the test comes back positive because of an applicant's use of prescription drugs, the department can ask about and verify that prescription drug use but cannot use the condition for which the drugs are prescribed to reject an applicant. Use of illegal drugs, of course, is grounds for disqualification.

Physical Disabilities and the ADA

After the conditional offer of employment, applicants can be rejected for disabilities revealed in the medical or psychological exam, according to the ADA, as long as the disabilities are related to essential job functions and no reasonable accommodations exist that would make it possible for the applicant to function in the job. For instance, a potential corrections officer with a heart condition can reasonably be rejected on the basis of that disability. While officers don't spend their lives running down cell blocks and up two flights of stairs, their lives or the lives of fellow officers or inmates may

---

PSYCHOLOGICAL EVALUATION TIPS

Just one, and you've seen it before: be honest.

depend on their being able to do so at a moment's notice. The corrections department can't accommodate someone who can't safely undergo severe physical stress and still get the job done.

Police and corrections departments have the right, even under the ADA, to reject applicants who have disabilities as minor as color blindness. Being able to provide descriptions of victims, suspects, vehicles and so on, both for investigative purposes and in court, is an essential function of a police officer, and there isn't always someone else available to make the identification.

If you've gotten this far, you don't have any obvious or seriously disabling conditions. You got through the written exam, physical agility test, psychological evaluation and interviews. Any other conditions that you reveal at this point or that come up in the medical exam will probably have to be dealt with on a case-by-case basis. Even conditions such as diabetes or epilepsy need not disqualify you, if your condition is controlled so that you will be able to fulfill the essential functions of an officer.

WHAT THE MEDICAL EXAM IS LIKE

The medical exam itself is nothing to be afraid of. It will be just like any other thorough physical exam. The doctor may be on the staff of the hiring agency or someone outside the department with his or her own practice, just like your own doctor. Your blood pressure, temperature, weight and so on will be measured; your heart and lungs will be listened to and your limbs examined. The doctor will peer into your eyes, ears, nose and mouth but it won't be that painful. You'll also have to donate some blood and some urine. Because of those tests, you won't know the results of the physical exam right away. You'll probably be notified in writing in a few weeks, after the test results come in.

IF AT FIRST YOU DON'T SUCCEED, PART ONE

The selection process for law enforcement officers is a rigorous one. If you fail one of the steps, take time for some serious self-evaluation.

If you fail the written test, look at the reasons you didn't do well. Was it just that the format was unfamiliar? Well, now you know what to expect.

Do you need to brush up on some of the skills tested? There are lots of books out there to help people with reading, writing and computation. You might start with the LearningExpress Skill Builders for Test Takers (order information at the back of this book). Enlist a teacher or a friend to help you, or check out the inexpensive courses offered by local high schools and community colleges.

Many agencies allow you to retest after a waiting period—a period you should use to improve your skills. If the exam isn't being offered again for years, consider trying some other jurisdiction.

If you fail the physical agility test, your course of action is clear. Increase your daily physical exercise until you *know* you can do what is required, and then retest or try another jurisdiction.

If you fail the oral board, try to figure out what the problem was. Do you think your answers were good but perhaps you didn't express them well? Then you need some practice in oral communication. You can take courses or enlist your friends to help you practice.

Did the questions and situations throw you for a loop, so you made what now seem like inappropriate answers? Then try to bone up for the next time. Talk to candidates who were successful and ask them what they said. Talk with officers you know about what might have been good answers for the questions you were asked. Even if your department doesn't allow you to redo the oral board, you can apply what you learn in applying to another department.

If the medical exam eliminates you, you will usually be notified as to what condition caused the problem. Is the condition one that can be corrected? See your doctor for advice. A few minor conditions can eliminate you in one jurisdiction but be acceptable in another. Contact the recruiting officer at a nearby department to see if you can apply there.

If you don't make the list and aren't told why, the problem might have been the oral board or, more likely, the psychological evaluation or the background investigation. Now you really have to do some hard thinking.

Can you think of *anything* in your past that might lead to questions about your fitness to be a law enforcement officer? Could any of your personal traits or attitudes raise such questions? And then the hard question: is there anything you can do to change these aspects of your past or your personality? If so, you might have a chance when you reapply or apply to another department. If not, it's time to think about another field.

If you feel you were wrongly excluded on the basis of a psychological evaluation or background check, most departments have appeals procedures. However, that word *wrongly* is very important. The psychologist or background investigator almost certainly had to supply a rationale in recommending against you. Do you have solid factual evidence that you can use in an administrative hearing to counter such a rationale? If not, you'd be wasting your time and money, as well as the hiring agency's, by making an appeal. Move carefully and get legal advice before you take such a step.

THE WAITING GAME

You went through the whole long process, passed all the tests, did the best you could, made the eligibility list—and now you wait. You *could* just sit on your hands. Or

you could decide to *do* something with this time to prepare for what you hope is your new career. Even if you don't get called, even if your rank on the score doesn't get you a job this time, you'll be better qualified for the next try. The chapters in this book on the individual law enforcement professions discuss ways to make yourself a more attractive candidate.

Here's one thing you *don't* want to do while you're waiting: Don't call to find out what your chances are or how far down on the list they've gotten or when they might call you. You probably won't get to talk to the people making those decisions, so you'll just annoy some poor receptionist. If you did get through to the decision-makers, you'd be in even worse shape: you'd be annoying *them.*

IF AT FIRST YOU DON'T SUCCEED, PART TWO

If you make the list, go through the waiting game and finally aren't selected, don't despair. Think through all the steps of the selection process, and use them to do a critical self-evaluation.

Maybe your written, physical or oral board score was high enough to pass but not high enough to put you near the top of the list. At the next testing, make sure you're better prepared.

Maybe you had an excellent score that should have put you at the top of the list, and you suspect that you were passed over for someone lower down. That means someone less well qualified was selected while you were not, right? Maybe, maybe not.

There were probably a lot of people on the list, and a lot of them may have scored high. One more point on the test might have made the difference, or maybe the department had the freedom to pick and choose on the basis of other qualifications. Maybe, in comparison with you, a lot of people on your list had more education or experience. Maybe there was a special need for people with particular skills, like proficiency in Spanish or Cantonese or training in photography. And yes, members of minority groups may have been given preference in hiring. Whether or not you think that's fair, you can be assured that it was a conscious decision on the part of the hiring agency; it may even have been mandated from above.

What can you do? You've heard or read about a lot of suits being brought against law enforcement agencies about their selection processes, particularly in large cities. That's a last resort, a step you would take only after getting excellent legal advice and thinking through the costs of time, money and energy. You'd also have to think about whether you'd want to occupy a position you got as the result of a lawsuit and whether you'd be hurting your chances of being hired somewhere else.

Most people are better off simply trying again. And don't limit your options. There are lots of police departments all over the country; there are city, county and state corrections agencies; there are other careers in law enforcement. Do your research. This book is a good start. Find out what's available. Find out who's hiring. Being turned down by one department need not be the end of your law enforcement career.

IF YOU DO SUCCEED

Congratulations! The end of the waiting game for municipal police and state trooper candidates (and, in some cases, for corrections officers, too) is notification to attend the academy. You're on the road to your law enforcement career.

The road is hardly over, though. In most jurisdictions, you're now hired as a recruit or trainee. You'll usually be paid to go to academy, though at a lower rate than you'll make when you actually become a member of the force. Academies typically run some 4–30 weeks—more for police, less for corrections—and include physical and firearms training as well as courses in techniques and procedures specific to your career. In many jurisdictions, the academy is followed by a period of field training in the jurisdiction that hired you.

After training, many states require law enforcement recruits to pass a certification exam. (Some jurisdictions even require that you be certified *before* you apply for a job.) The certification exam is usually directly related to the academy curriculum, so you'll know exactly what you need to study. And you *will* need to study; these exams are tough. But if you pass, your reward is the job you've worked so hard to get.

LAW ENFORCEMENT EDUCATION & TRAINING

7

CHAPTER SUMMARY

Demonstrating your capacity and desire to learn can put you a step ahead in being hired as a law enforcement officer and can keep you counted as a valuable member of the team once you're on board. What you'll learn in this chapter is something about current practices and trends related to educating and training law enforcement officers. This includes a look at higher education, academy and field training for new officers, and training programs for experienced officers.

o succeed as a law enforcement officer, one of the best things you can do is to involve yourself in learning right from the start. It's important to take advantage of every opportunity that comes your way to learn new skills and knowledge that will serve you well on the job—before you even apply, when you're first learning the ropes, and for as long as you're in the profession.

Just think about it. When departments are hiring, it's a sure bet that they'll focus on the most highly qualified and capable candidates. They need recruits who can quickly get up to speed in many different areas, whether it's learning self-defense techniques or learning about the legal system. They'll be looking for solid evidence that you're that kind of candidate, especially when the competition is steep.

Once you're selected as a recruit, the testing and evaluating continues. That's when you'll go through a demanding course of training, often for several weeks or months in a classroom setting and definitely on the job or in the field. To get hired and stay hired, you have to show the department how much you can learn and how well you can perform.

After you become a full-fledged member of a department, there's plenty of learning to do throughout your entire career. A lot of time, money and effort goes into educating and training police officers, state troopers, corrections officers and other law enforcement and criminal justice professionals. Departments have to make sure that officers are armed with all the up-to-date skills and knowledge they need to do their job effectively.

All in all, you're bound to stand out as an applicant, a recruit and an officer if you're always ready, willing and able to learn.

The College Debate

Having a college education has long been considered a "good to have" but not a "must have" qualification for becoming a police (including state police) or corrections officer. This position was taken a step farther in 1967 when a report from the President's Commission on Law Enforcement and the Administration of Justice made an official recommendation that *all* law enforcement officers hold a bachelor's degree.

Many experts in the field, then and now, have supported this recommendation. Within the federal government, you'll find a relatively high percentage of law enforcement jobs that require at least some college, if not a degree. It's still true that most municipal and state police departments across the U.S. do not require applicants to have more than a high school diploma or its equivalent. But it's also true that an increasing number of municipal and state police departments are adopting formal policies requiring some higher education for entry-level candidates and to be promoted down the road. New York City, for example, increased its minimum education requirement for police officers in 1996; applicants must have at least two years of college, or a high school diploma and two years of military service, to be hired.

Here's something else to consider. Whether or not departments actually have entry-level higher education requirements, many do end up hiring applicants who have some college education over those who don't. This isn't a matter of preferential treatment. It's simply that these applicants are often the ones who rank highest at the end of the selection process. For police officers in particular, these findings were backed up by a landmark study conducted by the Police Executive Research Forum (PERF), which was published in 1988. Over 347 municipal police departments nationwide were surveyed for this study, as well as smaller numbers of state police agencies, sheriff's departments and consolidated countywide police departments. In total, these agencies represented roughly 175,000 sworn law enforcement officers.

The PERF study not only showed the increasing importance of higher education in getting hired and promoted as a police officer; it also showed how many officers have been taking this message seriously. One dramatic statistic showed that in the years between 1970 and 1988, the number of officers with no college education dropped by half. More specifically, in 1970, 70% of officers nationwide had no college education and fewer than 1 in 20 held bachelor's degrees. But as of 1988, less than 35% had no college education; nearly 1 in 4 held bachelor's degrees; and another 42% had some years of college among their credentials. These numbers marked a clear trend toward a more highly educated police force. And that trend is still going strong.

Compared to police agencies, corrections department at the state and local level are implementing higher education requirements for new hires at a slower pace. Still, the American Correctional Association and other professional groups continue to push the increasing importance of higher education in this field. The job of a corrections officer today requires a "thinker's cap" to provide guidance to inmates, to communicate with an inmate population that is ethnically and culturally diverse, and to assist in rehabilitation efforts. In addition, as high-tech security systems become more widely used, there's a growing need for corrections officers to be skilled at operating these systems.

Even at state or local corrections facilities that don't require it, higher education gives you an advantage in getting hired and an even greater advantage in getting promoted to managerial positions. If you're applying to federal institutions, you'll face stricter terms right off the bat. The Federal Bureau of Prisons requires entry-level corrections officers to have either a four-year college degree or at least three years of work experience in law enforcement or corrections. In any case, earning some college credits can only work in your favor, never against.

Why the Focus on College?

Not everyone plans to or wants to attend college. Nor does having a college education, in and of itself, guarantee that a candidate will be a better police or corrections officer. Even so, college often does bring out certain traits that are key to the job and departments do take that into account in the selection process.

Put yourself in the shoes of a recruiting officer for a moment. You've got a pile of applications on your desk and some of them are from people who attended college. One thing to consider about these applicants is that they made a commitment; they were responsible enough to show up for classes and studious enough to pass their finals. They had to listen to lectures, participate in class discussions and projects, read books, write papers, take tests—all of which likely improved their communication and problem-solving skills.

These few factors alone say a lot. Police and corrections officers need to be responsible and disciplined. They are constantly communicating in a variety of ways and with a variety of people. Police officers take orders from their commanding officers, interview witnesses and suspects, review intelligence or procedural briefings. Corrections officers likewise take orders from their supervisors; they also explain the rules and regulations to inmates, instruct inmates in their work assignments, and review memos and reports on institutional policies and legal issues. Both police and corrections officers constantly write reports that need to be as detailed and logically constructed as possible, especially when criminal cases or parole hearings are hinging on them.

Of course, people can gain similar qualities without ever going to college, for example, through their life experiences, work background or military training. Neither police nor corrections departments overlook this fact when they're selecting applicants. But they also must consider that the college experience offers an atmosphere of learning and growth that can later benefit officers on the job. This is especially important as policing and corrections become more sophisticated in the methods and technologies used to perform their job duties.

Linking College to the Real World

By most accounts, law enforcement agencies tend to look favorably on candidates with a college education in any field of study. The particular knowledge that can come from a number of different disciplines—psychology, foreign languages, computer science, communications, sociology, public administration—can be useful to police and corrections work in various ways. Beyond the book learning, there's value in simply being exposed to new ways of thinking and to people from different walks of life.

You may be assuming that the best college education for police recruits to have would be in a field related specifically to policing, for example, a degree in criminal justice or police sciences. If policing is what you want to do, this can be a great route to take. It's even better if the college you want to attend has a good working relationship with the police department you'd like to join. The same goes for corrections officers: enrolling in classes or going for a degree in a college-level corrections program can serve you well on the job.

Many colleges are now partnering with law enforcement agencies to help keep their curriculum relevant to what's going on in the "real world." Police and corrections officers are being consulted about current issues, strategies and methods. College faculty are being brought in to teach classes at academies or to conduct training programs for experienced officers. New college courses are being developed that focus on particular needs of police or corrections departments in their geographic region. Some departments even offer college

credits for inservice training programs (that is, programs for full-duty, experienced officers, those who are already "in service").

These are some of the ways in which colleges with criminal justice programs are trying to "get real" in their educational efforts. If you're thinking about enrolling in college, go for the quality of the education first in any field of study. If you're thinking about taking courses specifically related to law enforcement or criminal justice, check out whether any colleges in your area are working together with police or corrections departments. You might get ahead of the game not only with the classes you take, but also with the network of contacts you make. (See the end of this chapter for a list of colleges in your state that offer law enforcement and/or criminal justice programs.)

Motivate to Educate

At municipal and state police departments, educational incentives are becoming a widespread means to support higher education in the ranks. These come in the form of policies or programs, formal and informal, that are aimed at encouraging officers to sign up for college classes or pursue a degree. Over 90% of the depart-

---

LEARNING THE SYSTEM

Here's a sampling of typical courses you could take through a college or university criminal justice program:
- Introduction to the Criminal Justice System
- Criminal Law
- Theories and Patterns of Criminal Behavior
- Criminal Rights and Procedures
- Law Enforcement in the U.S.
- Juvenile Justice System
- Security and Surveillance
- Criminal Investigation

ments interviewed for the 1988 PERF study already had at least one such policy or program in place, and many more departments have since joined the crowd.

A typical educational incentive offers to pay part or all of the tuition costs for college classes (successfully completed, of course). Another policy showing up in more and more departments, especially in urban areas, provides additional income or "education pay." For example, extra pay is often offered to motivate sworn officers to learn a second language that is common among citizens in their area. Some departments assist by allowing officers to adjust their work shifts and schedules so that they can attend classes. Others offer scholarships or other financial incentives not only for college classes, but also for advanced state certification courses and certain inservice training programs.

Most of the time, educational incentives are granted for coursework or training that is job-related. Departments may spell out what they consider to be "job-related" in a detailed formal policy, or they may approve courses on a case-by-case basis. Some incentives may apply to individual courses and others to full college degree programs. The most obvious conditions have to do with incentives being granted only when officers earn either a passing grade for pass/fail classes or a specific grade (such as a "B" or better) for graded classes; or maintain a certain grade point average (such as a 3.0 on a 4.0 scale) for a course of study or degree program.

Training Police Recruits

When new recruits are selected to join a police force, employment generally is conditional based on their passing a comprehensive training program run through a police academy. This training consists of classroom instruction in a broad range of subjects along with "hands-on" instruction to build certain physical and technical skills.

The exact curriculum and number of hours of instruction may vary among different police academies, but they usually address similar subject and skill areas. For example, at the onset of training, class time is often devoted to an overview of the U.S. criminal justice system. This may cover both law enforcement agencies and the courts, and could include a look at both the history of policing and modern policing strategies, challenges and responsibilities.

The law and criminal procedure are an important part of the academy curriculum. Specific areas of the law are covered, such as constitutional law and penal, civil, juvenile, and vehicle/traffic law. Police discretionary powers and the use of physical force are other common subjects. The more personal side of policing—interacting with the public, handling the pressures of the job and so forth—may be addressed through class topics like community relations and services, police ethics and stress management.

A large share of an academy's classroom instruction focuses on police procedures. To give you an idea of the depth and scope of information typically covered, see the accompanying sidebar that details this segment of the basic training course approved by the New York State Bureau for Municipal Police, Division of Criminal Justice Services. (The curriculum at a state police academy would cover much of the same material, but the focus may be greater in certain areas. For example, there may be relatively more attention paid to high-speed pursuit driving and handling road emergencies.)

Skills training makes up another major portion of a police academy course. Recruits must become adept in the use of firearms and other police weapons and equipment. They participate in a rigorous physical fitness program and receive instruction in self-defense, physical restraint and arrest techniques. They

POLICE PROCEDURES
A SAMPLE ACADEMY CURRICULUM

Patrol Functions (67 hours)
- Observation & Patrol
- Field Note-Taking
- Report Writing
- Intoxication
- Domestic Violence
- Mental Illness
- Alcoholic Beverage Control
- Nature & Control of Civil Disorder
- Bombs and Bomb Threats
- Crimes in Progress
- Police Communications
- Fingerprinting and Booking Procedures

Traffic (33 hours)
- Traffic Enforcement
- Impaired Driving
- Vehicle Pullovers
- Traffic Direction and Control

- Accident Investigation
- Hazardous Material Incidents

Criminal Investigation (44 hours)
- Preliminary Investigation and Information Development
- Interviews and Interrogations
- Physical Evidence
- Injury and Death Cases
- Larceny and Theft Cases
- Auto Theft
- Burglary Cases
- Robbery Cases
- Narcotics and Dangerous Drugs
- Organized Crime
- Sex Crimes
- Arson
- Case Preparation and Courtroom Demeanor

also learn to administer basic medical treatment and other forms of emergency assistance.

Police academy training is often sponsored by individual police departments—meaning they pay the bills for their recruits to attend. In recent years, however, community colleges in several states have begun to administer police academy programs (sometimes called "open enrollment academies").

The content and mission of these community college programs are like those of department-sponsored academies: aimed at preparing students for police work. The entrance requirements also tend to be similar, though students may need to first take certain college courses in areas such as English composition or

basic criminal law as a prerequisite. The main difference, however, is that you'll be taking on the financial responsibility yourself. Usually this includes registration and administrative fees plus costs for books, equipment, weapons, uniforms and other gear. (Costs vary by institution, but plan on a total of roughly $1,400 to $1,800.) What you get in return is certification as a police officer and proof that you've got what it takes to do the job.

Be aware, too, that some states require peace officers (police, corrections and other law enforcement officers) to be certified before they even apply for the job. Make sure you find out the requirements in your area by contacting the recruiting office of the department(s) where you'd like to work.

Training Corrections Officers

As with police officers, when you're first hired as a corrections officer, you will be considered a probationary employee and then will begin training. Federal, state and local corrections departments use training guidelines set by certain professional organizations, including the American Correctional Association and American Jail Association. What varies from institution to institution is whether you'll receive mostly on-the-job training or first go through a formal training program, such as an academy.

Many state corrections facilities send new officers to special academies or regional training centers. In some cases, this academy training is required as part of a certification process. Increasingly, formal programs are being adopted by more states and are also being used by local facilities such as county or city jails.

Academy training can last for several weeks or a few months. Classroom instruction may cover topics such as inmate behavior patterns, counseling inmates, managing conflict, dealing with cultural and ethnic diversity, contraband control, inmate rights, custody and security procedures, fire and safety techniques, written and oral communications. You also would undergo physical fitness training and develop certain technical skills, including the use of firearms and chemical weapons, self-defense, restraint tactics, first aid and emergency procedures.

Any formal training you receive will then be followed by on-the-job training, which takes place under the supervision of experienced corrections officers. This is where you'll put your knowledge and skills into practice, plus find out more about your institution's regulations and policies. Even if the facility you work for does not send you to an academy or training center, you will be taught the basic skills and knowledge you need through on-the-job training and may attend formal courses as needed.

If you're hired to work for the federal prison system, you will receive formal training through the Federal Bureau of Prisons (FBP). This includes 2 weeks of training at the institution that employs you and 3 weeks of basic correctional instruction at the FBP training center in Glynco, Georgia. This formal instruction is then followed by a period of supervised on-the-job training.

At all institutions—federal, state and local—it is common for corrections officers to participate in formal training courses after they've been on the job for awhile. Generally this inservice training is designed to teach officers new ideas and techniques or certain specialized skills, often for advancement in the job.

Policing in the Field

Offering some sort of field training has become regular practice among municipal and state police departments across the country. For some departments, this consists primarily of on-the-job training supervised by experienced senior-level officers. In recent years, however, many departments have implemented formal field training programs. These enable recruits to each receive the same level of training and be evaluated according to the same criteria.

This is especially the trend among municipal police departments. The number of formal programs began to increase as of the mid-1980s after the Commission on Accreditation for Law Enforcement Agencies, Inc. (CALEA), the country's only police accrediting agency, published training standards that included formal field training as a requirement for accreditation. This requirement was then approved by four prominent law enforcement organizations: the Police Executive Research Forum, the International Association of Chiefs of Police, the National Association of Black Law Enforcement Executives, and the National Sheriffs' Association.

Field training typically takes place after recruits have completed their police academy program, though some academies consider this to be the final phase of their program. Its main purpose is to provide practical experience in policing. Recruits are tested in actual situations, for example, conducting preliminary crime scene investigations, interviewing witnesses, making arrests and performing high-speed vehicle pursuits. On the whole, departments include the time spent on field training as part of the probationary employment period for new officers. Because you would still be "on probation," the evaluation of your performance in the field has a major bearing on whether you ultimately become a full-duty, sworn member of the force.

When you're participating in either formal programs or supervised on-the-job training, departments have the chance to gauge both your technical skills and your knowledge of laws and procedures gained from classroom instruction. Another critical part of the evaluation involves more subjective traits, such as your ability to manage crisis situations or to communicate effectively with different types of people.

Keep That Training Coming

Neither policing nor corrections were ever "easy" professions. Danger and stress have always come with the territory, just as mental alertness, physical stamina and emotional stability have always been vital traits for good officers. Still, it's safe to say that the challenges posed by modern society have made ongoing training and education more important for law enforcement officers than ever before.

Many departments tackle this need through specialized inservice training programs. These programs may cover specific procedures, such as riot control techniques or the use of new technologies and equipment. For a police department, they may highlight particular types of crime, such as situations involving drunk driving, bomb threats, violence against women, or bias and hate crimes. For a corrections department, they may highlight topics such as the effects of incarceration on behavior, substance abuse treatment, methods of rehabilitation, or nonviolent means of settling disputes.

Also popular now are training and education programs that address the "people side" of policing and corrections. To support local community policing efforts, for example, many police departments have devised programs around topics such as cultural diversity, conflict resolution, problem-solving, and teamwork. For state police officers, too, developing skills in such areas relative to their job can have a major impact on how well they interact with the public they serve and with fellow officers. Taking a different slant, similar topics are being addressed in training programs for corrections officers, but with the focus on their interaction with inmates.

Many departments make use of outside agencies and organizations for continued training and education. As noted earlier, colleges are a regular source for program development and faculty assistance. Several state and federal agencies, such as the Federal Bureau of Investigation (FBI), make some of their law enforcement programs available to municipal or state police forces and corrections departments.

Professional associations are another valuable resource. The International Association of Chiefs of Police (IACP), for example, has long offered various management training and self-help programs to police administrators and officers. The American Society of Law Enforcement Trainers (ASLET) regularly sponsors "Train the Trainer" and other programs to foster high quality training standards and practices in the profession.

Individual officers and entire departments alike can benefit from outside resources like these. They can be particularly helpful to small departments, which may not have the funding or personnel needed to run their own training programs.

High-Tech Training for Police

In policing, as with most professions today, high-tech advancements are changing the way police officers do their jobs. Police cars are being equipped with notebook computers and sophisticated communications devices. Officers are writing their reports on keyboards instead of clipboards. On-line data bases are being tapped to get instant information from statewide, national and international law enforcement agencies. Learning *about* technology is becoming a necessity for police officers. But they also can learn *through* technology.

Numerous high-tech methods of training and educating officers already exist and are bound to become more widely used in the future. One example is computer-based training, which offers an interactive means for officers to learn at their own pace. Instead of being run through mock physical trials or tested in actual street situations, they can check their reactions and decisions through computer simulations of crimes in progress or emergency circumstances.

Teleconferencing systems are another means of delivering training programs. These systems enable departments to download and broadcast educational videos to officers in different geographic locations at the same time. They also allow for televised training courses in which "class members" can talk back and forth with instructors and each other no matter where they are located. Such programs already are being provided through law enforcement organizations such as the FBI and the California Peace Officer Standards

and Training (POST) commission. The corporate world is making a contribution, too. Radio Shack, for example, was honored in 1995 by the Crime Prevention Coalition for its "United Against Crime" program that provides interactive satellite-beamed training courses to law enforcement and community activists nationwide.

Learn to Earn

To successfully carry out their particular mission, every police department, corrections department and other law enforcement agency must ensure that officers are performing up to their full potential. They need to provide officers with the right set of tools for the job. That's basically what happens through education and training.

You can pursue any number of educational efforts on your own. You can take full advantage of training offered through the department or institution you work for. Through both these routes, you'll be helping yourself to meet the ever-changing challenges of your profession for a long time to come.

If You're College Bound . . .

To give yourself an edge in getting hired as a law enforcement officer, you can't go wrong by getting a college education. More and more state and local police departments are requiring college credits to apply and, later on, for officers to get promoted. Many other law enforcement agencies—police, state police and corrections departments—treat higher education as a factor that sets you apart in the selection process and to advance in the ranks later on. Either way, you stand to gain by adding higher education to your resume.

The following pages list two- and four-year colleges in New York State that offer criminal justice programs. Some of these programs are Bachelor's or Associate degrees in criminal justice or in Corrections. Some community colleges also operate a police academy training program. You could sign up for a few classes or go for a full two-year (Associate) or four-year (Bachelor's) degree. A college admissions department can give you information about course offerings and degree requirements.

The other department you'll want to contact is financial aid. Funding is available from a variety of sources—grants and loans from the federal government; institutional aid, work-study programs and scholarships through the colleges; plus grants, scholarships and endowments from private organizations. Many students wind up with a combination of grants, which don't have to be repaid, and loans, which do. Remember, though, that student loans are generally made with favorable interest rates and repayment plans.

A financial aid officer can help you sort through your options and complete the necessary paperwork to apply for funding. Also do some investigating on your own. Spend some time at the library scanning the many directories and other reference materials that are published on the subject. Contact professional organizations, too. Numerous scholarships are out there specifically for students pursuing law enforcement careers. Funds are often available from both private and government sources for members of certain minority or ethnic groups, or for military veterans, for example, through the GI Bill.

The main thing to keep in mind about getting a college education is that it's an investment in your career. That's clearly a good cause.

FOUR-YEAR SCHOOLS OFFERING CRIMINAL JUSTICE DEGREE PROGRAMS

Alfred University
Saxon Drive
Alfred, NY 14802
800-541-9229
607-871-2115
Bachelor's in Criminal Justice
Scholarships available

Elmira College
Park Place
Elmira, NY 14901
800-935-6472
607-735-1724
Bachelor's in Criminal Justice
Scholarships available

Fordham University
East Fordham Road
Bronx, NY 10458
800-FORDHAM
718-817-4000
Bachelor's in Criminal Justice
Scholarships available

Hilbert College
5200 South Park Avenue
Hamburg, NY 14075
716-649-7900
Associate and Bachelor's in Criminal Justice
Scholarships available

Iona College
715 North Avenue
New Rochelle, NY 10801
914-633-2502
Bachelor's in Criminal Justice
Scholarships available

John Jay College of Criminal Justice
899 Tenth Avenue
New York, NY 10019-1093
212-237-8865
Bachelor's in Criminal Justice, Police Science,
Criminal Justice Administration. Associate in
Correction Administration, Police Science.
Scholarships available

Long Island University, C.W. Post Campus
Brookville, NY 11548
516-299-2413
Bachelor's in Criminal Justice
Scholarships available for continuing students only

Marist College
290 North Road
Poughkeepsie, NY 12601
914-575-3226
Bachelor's in Criminal Justice
Scholarships available

Mercy College
Dobbs Ferry, NY 10522
914-693-7600
Bachelor's in Criminal Justice
Scholarships available

Niagara University
Niagara University, NY 14109
800-462-2111
716-286-8700
Bachelor's in Criminal Justice
Scholarships available

Pace University
Pleasantville/Briarcliff Campus
Pleasantville, NY 10570
914-773-3746
Bachelor's in Criminal Justice
Scholarships available

Roberts Wesleyan College
2301 West Side Drive
Rochester, NY 14624
800-777 4RWC
716-594-4600
Bachelor's in Criminal Justice
Scholarships available

Rochester Institute of Technology
One Lomb Memorial Drive
Rochester, NY 14623
716-475-6631
Bachelor's in Criminal Justice
Scholarships available

St. John's University
800 Utopia Parkway
Jamaica, NY 11439
718-990-6240
Bachelor's in Criminal Justice
Scholarships available

St. Joseph's College, New York
245 Clinton Avenue
Brooklyn, 11205-3688
718-636-6868
Certificate in Criminal Justice
Scholarships available

St. Thomas Aquinas College
Sparkill, NY 10976
914-398-4100
Bachelor's in Criminal Justice
Scholarships available

State University of New York at Brockport
350 New Campus Drive
Brockport, NY 14420
716-395-2751
Bachelor's in Criminal Justice
Scholarships available

State University of New York at Buffalo
1300 Elmwood Avenue
Buffalo, NY 14222
716-878-4017
Bachelor's in Criminal Justice
Scholarships available

State University of New York at Fredonia
Fredonia, NY 14063
800-252-1212
716-673-3251
Bachelor's in Criminal Justice
Scholarships available

State University of New York at Plattsburgh
101 Broad Street
Plattsburgh, NY 12901
518-564-2040
Bachelor's in Criminal Justice
Scholarships available

State University of New York at Oswego
Oswego, NY 13126
315-341-2250
Bachelor's in Criminal Justice
Scholarships available

State University of New York at Albany
1400 Washington Avenue
Albany, NY 12222
518-442-5435
Bachelor's in Criminal Justice
Scholarships available

Utica College of Syracuse University
1600 Burrstone Road
Utica, NY 13502
800-782-8884
315-792-3006
Bachelor's in Criminal Justice
Scholarships available

TWO-YEAR SCHOOLS OFFERING AN ASSOCIATE DEGREE IN CORRECTIONS AND/OR CRIMINAL JUSTICE

Canton College of Technology
Cornell Drive
Canton, NY 13617
800-388-7123
315-386-7123
Associate in Criminal Justice, Corrections
Police Academy

Cayuga County Community College
Auburn, NY 13021
315-255-1743
Associate in Corrections, Criminal Justice
Scholarships available

Clinton Community College
Plattsburgh, NY 12901
518-562-4175
Associate in Criminal Justice
Scholarships available

Columbia-Green Community College
4400 Route 23
Hudson, NY 12534
518-828-5513
Associate in Criminal Justice
Scholarships available

Corning Community College
Corning, NY 14830
607-962-9220
Associate in Criminal Justice
Scholarships available

Dutchess Community College
53 Pendell Road
Poughkeepsie, NY 12601
914-431-8010
Associate in Criminal Justice

Erie Community College, City Campus
Main Street and Young's Road
Williamsville, NY 14221
716-851-1455
Associate in Criminal Justice
Scholarships available

Erie Community College, North Campus
6205 Main Street
Williamsville, NY 14221
716-851-1455
Associate in Criminal Justice
Scholarships available

Finger Lakes Community College
4355 Lake Shore Drive
Canandaigua, NY 14424
716-394-3500
ext. 278
Associate in Criminal Justice

Fulton-Montgomery Community College
2805 State Highway 67
Johnstown, NY 12095
518-762-4651
Associate in Criminal Justice
Scholarships available

Genesee Community College
1 College Road
Batavia, NY 14020
716-343-0055
Associate in Criminal Justice
Scholarships available

Herkimer County Community College
100 Reservoir Road
Herkimer, NY 13350
800-947-4432
315-866-0300
Associate in Corrections, Criminal Justice
Police Academy
Scholarships available

Hudson Valley Community College
80 Vandenburgh Avenue
Troy, New York 12180
518-270-7309
Associate in Criminal Justice
Scholarships available

Jamestown Community College
525 Falconer Road
Jamestown, NY 14701
800-388-8557
716-665-5220
Associate in Criminal Justice
Police Academy
Scholarships available

Jefferson Community College
Outer Coffeen Street
Watertown, NY 13601
315-786-2408
Associate in Criminal Justice
Scholarships available

Mater Dei College
5428 State Highway 37
Ogdensburg, NY 13669
800-724-4080
315-393-5930
Associate in Criminal Justice

Mohawk Valley Community College
1101 Sherman Drive
Utica, NY 13501
315-792-5353
Associate in Criminal Justice
Scholarships available

Monroe Community College
1000 East Henrietta Road
Rochester, NY 14623-5780
716-292-2200
Associate in Corrections, Criminal Justice
Police Academy
Scholarships available

Nassau Community College
Garden City, NY 11530-6793
516-572-7345
Associate in Criminal Justice
Scholarships available

Niagara County Community College
3111 Saunders Settlement Road
Sanborn, NY 14132-9460
716-731-3271
Associate in Criminal Justice
Scholarships available

North Country Community College
PO Box 89
Saranac Lake, NY 12983
518-891-2915
Associate in Criminal Justice

Onondaga Community College
4941 Onondaga
Syracuse, NY 13215
315-469-2201
Associate in Criminal Justice
Scholarships available

Orange County Community College
115 South Street
Middletown, NY 19400
914-341-4030
Associate in Criminal Justice

Sage Junior College of Albany
140 Scotland Avenue
Albany, NY 12208
800-999-9522
518-445-1730
Associate in Criminal Justice
Scholarships available

Schenectady County Community College
78 Washington Avenue
Schenectady, NY 12305
518-346-6211
Associate in Criminal Justice
Scholarships available

Suffolk County Community College
Ammerman Campus
Selden, NY 11784-2851
516-451-4022
Associate in Criminal Justice
Scholarships available after completion of 24 credits

Suffolk County Community College
Eastern Campus
Riverhead, NY 11901
516-548-2513
Associate in Criminal Justice
Scholarships available for continuing students

Suffolk County Community College
Western Campus
Brentwood, NY 11717
516-851-6704
Associate in Criminal Justice
Scholarships available for continuing students

Sullivan County Community College
Leroy Road
Loch Sheldrake, NY 12759
914-434-5750
Associate in Corrections, Criminal Justice
Police Academy
Scholarships available

Tompkins Cortland Community College
170 North Street
Dryden, NY 13530
607-844-8211
Associate in Criminal Justice
Scholarships available

Ulster County Community College
Stone Ridge, NY 12484
800-724-0833
914-687-5022
Associate in Criminal Justice
Scholarships available

Westchester Community College
75 Grasslands Road
Valhalla, NY 10595-1698
914-785-6735
Associate in Corrections, Criminal Justice
Police Academy
Most scholarships available for recent high school graduates

C · H · A · P · T · E · R

LAW ENFORCEMENT CAREERS

8

CHAPTER SUMMARY

The sky's the limit when it comes to job opportunities in the field of law enforcement. This chapter explores a wide range of career options, including information about job duties, requirements, training, and application and testing procedures.

f you want a career related to law enforcement, you won't be lacking in possibilities. From the U.S. government on down to private security firms, an enormous assortment of job opportunities is out there. Your main tasks will be deciding what kind of job you prefer and determining the qualifications you'll need to get hired.

Certain basic roles are common to many of the positions described in this chapter. These include preventing crime, keeping the peace, providing protection and security, enforcing the law, and investigating crimes. However, even if a particular job carries each of these responsibilities, one role may be emphasized more than another. For example, a special agent for the FBI may concentrate primarily on criminal investigations, while a special agent for the Secret Service may focus on setting up complex protection and security systems. Keep this in mind as you read these job descriptions and consider the work that interests you most.

Where you would be working is another consideration. Mostly outdoors or indoors? In a large metropolitan area? At a remote border post?

Will a job require you to relocate frequently? Will you spend a lot of time traveling across the U.S.? Or overseas?

You'll also want to think about the level of danger involved; the type of people you'll be encountering on the job; the diversity of your job duties; the type of special skills, knowledge and technical expertise you'll need to have or acquire. All in all, many factors will weigh into your choice of jobs to pursue. The information provided here simply gives you a good starting point in your decision-making and job-hunting process.

With regard to requirements and application procedures for these jobs, you'll find that some general guidelines apply to most. For instance, plan on having to be in good physical shape, a competent driver, and capable of passing a background check. Other attributes may not be specifically required—such as strong communication skills, computer training, related work experience, college education, a military background—but can improve your chances. Because there are often many more applicants than there are job openings, every extra advantage matters.

When you're exploring opportunities in this field, remember that each job could either become your lifelong profession or serve as a steppingstone to other careers. Maybe you'll decide to start out as a municipal police officer or state trooper, then move on to a federal law enforcement position. The point is, the experience you gain in one area of law enforcement usually can be put to good use in another. You don't have to limit your choices to just one job in your lifetime—though you may need to choose one job at a time.

COPS, COURTS AND CORRECTIONS

This section offers job descriptions for the following positions:

- Deputy Sheriff
- Police Officer
- State Police Officer
- Court Officer
- Corrections Officer

DEPUTY SHERIFF
What You'll Do on the Job

Deputy Sheriffs serve as law enforcement agents for a county. While their duties are much like those of municipal and state police officers, they typically have a wider range of responsibilities involving the county courts and correctional facilities. (Note that many small towns may be served by a county sheriff's office rather than a municipal police department. Sheriffs, but not deputy sheriffs, are most often elected to, rather than hired for, that position.)

Deputy Sheriffs patrol assigned areas within their jurisdiction, enforce laws and maintain order. They investigate suspicious or criminal activity and have the authority to question, arrest and transport suspects, as well as to conduct searches and seize evidence. Another aspect of their job is to perform traffic control and crowd control. On county roads, Deputy Sheriffs may issue traffic citations and often provide emergency assistance, including administering first aid to accident victims and calling for ambulances and other emergency vehicles as needed. They may conduct standard criminal investigations, occasionally involving surveillance and undercover work.

For the county court system, Deputy Sheriffs may serve subpoenas, summonses, warrants and other court orders. Other court-authorized assignments include conducting evictions and confiscating property. They may escort prisoners to and from correctional facilities for courtroom appearances, sometimes across state lines, or for medical or attorney appointments.

They may also provide security inside courtrooms as well as in correctional facilities.

Qualifications

Different counties have different criteria for hiring Deputy Sheriffs. In most places, you must be between 21 and 29 years of age, a U.S. citizen, and have a valid driver's license. You will need a high school diploma or a General Equivalency Degree (GED) at the minimum; many sheriff's departments now include at least some college education in their requirements. In some areas you must pass a written exam (typically a civil service exam); in others your work history and/or a personal interview will be used for selection. You can expect to undergo physical performance tests, a medical exam, some form of psychological testing and a background investigation.

Training Involved

Training tends to vary even more than hiring requirements among different counties. Often the type and amount of training have to do with the size of the department. Smaller departments may opt for on-the-job training under close supervision by a superior officer, while larger departments may have formal training procedures lasting up to several months, followed by on-the-job training.

Applying for the Job

For information about application requirements and job openings, you can contact sheriff's departments directly. If civil service examinations are given in your state for this position, you may also be able to get information about application and testing procedures from state civil service commissions.

POLICE OFFICER
What You'll Do on the Job

Police Officers perform numerous law enforcement duties related primarily to maintaining law and order and protecting people and property. The majority of law enforcement jobs in this country are in municipal police departments.

Police Officers patrol the communities they serve by car, on foot or by other means of transportation. They watch for, investigate and attempt to prevent or disrupt suspicious or illegal activity. They respond to radio calls about various crimes committed or in progress—anything from burglaries or robberies to assaults, rapes, murders, and illegal drug trafficking. At the scene of a crime, they may question crime victims, witnesses or suspects, secure criminal evidence, and arrest suspects. While on patrol, Police Officers are also on the lookout for public safety hazards and may issue citations, or even make arrests, for various motor vehicle and parking violations.

Another major area of responsibility involves traffic and/or crowd control. Police Officers may carry out these tasks for planned public gatherings such as parades, political demonstrations, and sports events. They also perform these functions under emergency conditions, including auto accidents, explosions, fires and natural disasters, and may provide basic medical care to accident or crime victims.

Police Officers are highly trained in the use of physical force and weapons to subdue or apprehend criminals. In addition to preparing detailed written reports that can be used as evidence in criminal cases, they frequently provide court testimony during criminal trials.

Qualifications

Though requirements for becoming a Police Officer vary among police departments, typically you must be a U.S. citizen between the ages of 18 and 29 at the time of appointment. A valid driver's license and a good driving record are required. You must pass a written test, personal interview, background investigation, psychological testing, drug screening, physical performance tests, and a physical exam (including vision and hearing tests). A high school diploma or GED may meet the educational criteria. However, some college education may be required or preferred in the selection process. You may need to be a resident of the city or county in which you apply. If you have served in the military, you may receive what is known as "veterans preference points" on the written test.

Training Involved

Most Police Officer recruits undergo formal training in a police academy that lasts several weeks or months. This includes classroom instruction in subjects related to the law and law enforcement procedures as well as skills training, for example, in self-defense techniques and the use of firearms. New recruits also can expect a period of on-the-job or field training under the supervision of experienced officers. Employment generally is considered to be probationary based on successfully completing a department's designated course of training.

Applying for the Job

For information about application requirements and testing procedures, contact the personnel or recruiting office of the police department(s) where you want to apply.

STATE POLICE OFFICER
What You'll Do on the Job

The primary responsibility of State Police Officers (sometimes known as State Troopers) is to patrol and enforce laws that govern the use of state and interstate highways, turnpikes and freeways. In addition to enforc-

ing motor vehicle laws, they also may enforce criminal laws and assist other law enforcement agencies with criminal investigations, especially in counties without a local police force or a large sheriff's department. Ensuring public safety, providing emergency assistance and offering general assistance to motorists are other typical duties.

While on patrol, State Police Officers are on the lookout for motor vehicle violations, such as exceeding the speed limit, and any evidence of unsafe driving. They can stop motorists and check for valid driver's licenses, vehicle registrations and valid vehicle inspection stickers. This can include using computerized equipment to tap into state or interstate data bases and run identification and vehicle checks, for example, to determine if a vehicle is stolen or a driver is wanted for criminal violations. When justified, they can issue citations, search vehicles or make arrests.

State Police Officers frequently respond to the scene when emergencies occur on the highways such as car accidents or fires or when vehicles break down and block traffic. Depending on the situation, they may direct traffic, render first aid, call for emergency equipment or assist in other ways. The written reports and diagrams that these officers prepare when accidents occur are used for evidence in any subsequent legal proceedings. To maintain public safety on the highways, these officers also perform actions necessary to alleviate unsafe road conditions caused by road damage, debris on the roads, bad weather or other factors. State Police Officers commonly provide help to motorists in non-emergency situations as well, such as giving directions or offering information about local services and facilities.

Qualifications

Requirements for this position vary among the states, generally according to their prevailing civil service regulations. In most states, you must be a U.S. citizen between 21 and 29 years of age at the time of appointment and a resident of the state in which you are applying. Other typical requirements include passing a written test, personal interview, physical examination (including vision and hearing tests), physical performance tests, some form of psychological testing, possibly a polygraph and drug screening, and a thorough background investigation. A high school diploma or GED may satisfy the minimum educational requirements. Some level of college education may be required; in most states it serves as an advantage in the hiring process.

Training Involved

Selected recruits for State Police Officer positions participate in a formal training program, which may range in length from 3 to 4 months. This training covers general policing methods as well as subjects specific to this position. These include instruction in state motor vehicle codes, patrol and surveillance techniques, and pursuit driving. After completing this training, additional on-the-job training takes place under the supervision of experienced state police officers.

Applying for the Job

For information about application requirements and job openings, contact the state police department's personnel or recruiting office. State civil service commissions may also be able to provide information about application and testing procedures.

COURT OFFICER
What You'll Do on the Job

Court Officers (sometimes called "bailiffs") provide security and maintain order in federal, state, county and municipal courtrooms. It is their job to protect the judge, jury and others present during hearings and tri-

als; to ensure that courtroom proceedings are not interrupted; to conduct searches for illegal firearms or weapons; and to restrain prisoners or others who exhibit disruptive or violent behavior. They may serve as an escort to jurors, as well as guard sequestered jurors from outside contact. They may also escort and guard prisoners on trial.

In the courtroom, Court Officers act under the supervision of the judge. Usually they are the ones who call witnesses and defendants to the witness stand. They make sure that the courtroom is properly equipped, clean and orderly. They also may perform certain court-related administrative duties on a regular basis or at a judge's request.

Qualifications

Minimum job requirements for Court Officers differ from place to place. You can plan on taking a written test, such as a civil service examination, and going through a personal interview. You also can count on a high school diploma or GED requirement, with higher education always being a plus—and sometimes a must—for employment. Your communication skills and ability to interact well with others are important because of the variety of people you'll be dealing with—judges, lawyers, jurors, witnesses, defendants, reporters and other courtroom participants and visitors. Work experience that demonstrates these skills will put you a step ahead, as will any experience related to serving the courts.

Training Involved

Court Officers generally receive formal instruction and training, often through an academy, in areas such as court laws and procedures; state, federal and municipal laws, depending on the court where you'll be working; the use of firearms; self-defense techniques; and arrest procedures and techniques.

Applying for the Job

For information about career oppurtunities and application requirements and procedures for Court Officers, you can contact federal, state, county and municipal courthouses in your area or state. Federal and state government employment centers also post job openings for Court Officers.

CORRECTIONS OFFICER
What You'll Do on the Job

Corrections Officers guard and supervise prisoners confined to penal institutions. While this basic role doesn't change, their specific duties will vary depending on the size and type of institution—federal or state penitentiaries, city or county jails, reformatories or detention centers—and the level of security or supervision required by an institution (minimum or maximum security).

Corrections Officers monitor the behavior of inmates at all times to maintain order, enforce the rules of the institution, and prevent escape. They routinely search inmates and cells for prohibited items or materials. They also make sure that cells and outer facilities remain secure, for example, that locks, window bars or doors have not been tampered with. A constant duty is being on the lookout for any signs of tension or disruptive conduct among inmates which could lead to physical disputes or emergency situations such as riots.

The disciplinary role of Corrections Officers is vital and can involve the use of force or weapons. However, it is their further responsibility to *protect* inmates. They have a duty to ensure the health, safety and well-being of inmates while they are institutionalized; and, for those inmates who eventually will be released, help prepare them to lead productive lives outside the institution.

Qualifications

Employment requirements for Corrections Officers vary depending on the institution. In general, federal prisons, large institutions and/or maximum security facilities may have more stringent requirements than small and/or minimum security facilities. Most often, you must be at least 21 years old and have a high school diploma or a GED. Good physical health and emotional stability are standard criteria so you can expect some kind of medical, fitness and psychological testing. Polygraph (lie detector) tests, drug screening and background investigations are also common. You may or may not be required to pass a written test (such as a civil service examination). Related work experience and higher education rate highly in the hiring process; one or the other is required by some institutions, especially at federal institutions.

Training Involved

Corrections Officers in federal prisons receive formal training through the Federal Bureau of Prisons. On-the-job training directed by experienced officers is customary at the state and local level, often supplemented with specialized formal training courses. Many state facilities, however, have adopted or plan to adopt formal training programs like those conducted for federal institutions.

Applying for the Job

For information about career opportunities for corrections officers, you can contact correctional institutions and facilities in your area; state departments of corrections; state civil service commissions; the Federal Bureau of Prisons; or the Federal Office of Personnel Management (OPM). You may also want to contact national organizations in this field, such as The American Correctional Association, 8025 Laurel Lakes Ct., Laurel, MD 20707; and The International Association of Correctional Officers, Box 53, 1333 South Wabash Avenue, Chicago, IL 60605.

FEDERAL AGENCIES

The U.S. Government provides numerous opportunities for those interested in a law enforcement career. Many federal agencies, for example, maintain their own police forces and investigative or security units. Typically, each agency provides general law enforcement training, often through the Federal Law Enforcement Training Center in Glynco, Georgia, as well as specialized training relative to its particular mission (for example, to enforce federal immigration laws or drug laws, to ensure the safety of government officials, or to protect government property and lands). Whatever its mission or jurisdiction, these agencies frequently work in tandem, lending their expertise to criminal investigations or assisting each other in emergency situations.

Information on application and testing procedures is provided with the federal job descriptions that follow. Some federal agencies have the authority to test and hire applicants directly. As you'll see, many others work through the Office of Personnel Management (OPM) to fill job openings. When this is the case, the OPM typically accepts applications for employment with a specific federal agency; administers the appropriate written tests; and then submits an eligibility list of qualified candidates to the agency for consideration. (If you already work for a federal agency, you may be able to apply directly to another agency rather than go through the OPM.)

The OPM operates Federal Job Information/Testing Centers in major metropolitan areas across the country. When written tests are required by an agency that works through the OPM, these tests generally will be given at these centers. This is also where you can find out about current job openings and request the application forms you'll need. For a list of computerized job-search centers operated by the OPM across the country, plus federal job hotline numbers and other on-line services you can use, see the end of this chapter.

You can expect a lot of paperwork when you're applying for federal jobs—and it's crucial that you provide every piece of paper that's requested. Announcements that are made for federal job vacancies—for example, by the OPM or directly through a federal agency—indicate what information is needed to apply. For most federal jobs, you can apply using a resume, a form known as the Optional Application for Federal Employment (available through the OPM), or some similar kind of written statement. You also may be asked to send along other documents, such as a college transcript or a certificate of discharge from military service.

Keep in mind, too, that federal jobs are classified a certain way to indicate the experience, salary level and other features of the job. These classifications are known as "grades." With your application, you usually need to indicate the job title; the announcement number of the job; and the grade(s) assigned to the job.

The important point is that whatever paperwork you submit must contain *all* the information that is requested in a job vacancy announcement and on the Optional Application form. Otherwise, you may not be considered for the job. At the same time, don't send more information than they ask for! Keep your resume or application brief yet complete—and certainly legible and neat.

BUREAU OF ALCOHOL, TOBACCO AND FIREARMS

The Bureau of Alcohol, Tobacco and Firearms (ATF) is responsible for the administration and criminal enforcement of federal laws involving alcohol, tobacco, firearms and explosives. This includes ensuring that the government collects revenues due from legal trade within these industries. With regard to criminal activity, the agency serves to prevent the illegal possession, use and trafficking of such commodities as liquor, cigarettes and guns. Many bombing incidents and for-profit arson schemes also fall under this agency's jurisdiction.

SPECIAL AGENT
What You'll Do on the Job

Special Agents perform investigative work related to federal laws that are regulated by the ATF Bureau. They conduct investigations aimed at uncovering the illegal manufacture, possession, trafficking or smuggling of cigarettes and liquor. They investigate similar kinds of criminal activities with regard to firearms and explosives as well. Typical cases include arson and bombing incidents and the trafficking of guns, ammunition and bombing devices, which frequently involve organized crime or terrorist groups.

Special Agents also oversee and investigate entities that are legally engaged in trade in these industries. This includes monitoring the activities of commercial manufacturers, dealers and distributors of firearms, explosives and cigarettes, along with alcohol distilleries and breweries. The violations they uncover could range from illegal transport to tax fraud to bribery.

Depending on the type of case, Special Agents may set up surveillance operations, work undercover or instigate raids. Questioning informants, witnesses and suspects are key duties to gather information and physical evidence of violations. With proper legal warrants, Special Agents are authorized to conduct searches and seize contraband or physical evidence. In addition, they help prepare cases for criminal prosecution and give court testimony when needed.

Qualifications

Among other requirements for a Special Agent position, you must be a U.S. citizen between the ages of 21 and 37. You will need to take the Treasury Enforcement Agent (TEA) written examination. After passing the TEA exam, you then must pass a personal interview, a background investigation, drug screening and physical exam (including vision and hearing tests). A four-year degree from an accredited college or university is required. In some cases, the equivalent in work experience or education plus work experience may be considered instead.

Training Involved

As a Special Agent trainee, you'll receive eight weeks of training in general law enforcement and investigative techniques at the Federal Law Enforcement Training Center in Glynco, Georgia. This training includes courses in surveillance techniques, rules of evidence, undercover assignments, arrest and raid techniques and the use of firearms. Specialized training is later provided that covers the specific duties of ATF Special Agents, such as instruction related to laws enforced by the ATF Bureau, case report writing, firearms and explosives operations, bomb scene searches and arson investigations.

Applying for the Job

You may contact your local OPM area office regarding the TEA Examination, which is administered by the OPM. More information on testing and application procedures is available through the Bureau of Alcohol, Tobacco and Firearms, Personnel Division-Employment Branch, Washington, D.C. 20226. A job information line can be reached at 202-927-8610.

DRUG ENFORCEMENT ADMINISTRATION

Enforcing U.S. laws regarding illegal drug trafficking and preventing drug abuse are the chief responsibilities of the Drug Enforcement Administration (DEA). Through its investigative activities, the DEA seeks to track down major suppliers of narcotic and dangerous drugs both in the U.S. and abroad. Their efforts focus on the distribution of illicit drugs such as heroin, cocaine, hallucinogens and marijuana, as well as both illegal and legal trade in depressants, stimulants and other controlled substances. Research and public education are other important roles performed by the DEA to combat drug abuse.

SPECIAL AGENT
What You'll Do on the Job
DEA Special Agents aim to uncover criminal drug activities and apprehend violators of federal drug laws so that they can be brought to prosecution. Their major duties involve planning and conducting investigations that target suspected sources of supply. This includes individuals and organizations who produce and distribute illegal drugs and narcotics, and those who divert legal controlled substances for unlawful drug trade.

Special Agents coordinate their investigative efforts with other federal, state and local law enforcement agencies, especially to open the channels of information about methods used and people engaged in the illegal trafficking of drugs. They are heavily involved with the international community as well. Working with foreign governments, agencies and law enforcement officials, they help to develop intelligence networks, investigate unlawful drug trade, institute drug control and anti-drug abuse programs, and other such services.

Surveillance and undercover work are common in this profession. Because DEA Agents focus primarily on large-scale illegal drug operations, these endeavors can be highly dangerous. Their goal is to expose major suppliers and distributors before banned or addictive drugs can reach the user. They also enforce federal laws by monitoring the transactions of drug companies and other legitimate channels of narcotic and dangerous drugs.

Special Agents collect information through any paper trails available and by questioning informants, witnesses and suspects. When sufficient evidence and cause have been established, they are authorized to arrest suspects and confiscate illegal drug supplies. Their investigations are the basis for criminal trials, in which they assist by helping to prepare cases and by testifying in court. Special Agents also share their knowledge of drug control and drug-related crime by participating in various training, education and research endeavors.

Qualifications
Candidates for DEA Special Agent positions must be U.S. citizens between the ages of 21 and 35 at the time of appointment. Although no written test is required, you will need to pass a physical examination (including vision and hearing tests) and a thorough background investigation. Any form of drug abuse, past or present, would be grounds for immediate disqualification. To qualify, you must have a degree in any field from an accredited college or university and either (a) one year of work experience; or (b) an overall GPA of 2.5 on a 4.0 scale and a 3.5 GPA in your major field of study, with an academic standing in the upper ⅓ of a graduating class or major subdivision (for example, a college's school of business or division of arts and sciences), membership in a scholastic honor society, plus one year of graduate study.

Training Involved

Applicants for DEA Special Agent positions participate in 14 weeks of basic training at the FBI Academy in Quantico, Virginia. This training includes courses in narcotic laws, arrest techniques, surveillance techniques, search and seizure laws, firearms use, practical exercises and self-defense.

Applying for the Job

Applications should be sent directly to the nearest DEA office for hiring consideration. Certain forms and pieces of documentation must be provided with your application. This may include a resume or Optional Application for Federal Employment, a Background Survey Questionnaire (OPM Form 1386) and a completed college transcript. More information on testing and application procedures is available through the Drug Enforcement Administration, Office of Personnel, 1405 I Street N.W., Washington, D.C. 20537.

FEDERAL BUREAU OF INVESTIGATION

As its name implies, the chief responsibility of the Federal Bureau of Investigation (FBI) is to investigate violations of federal laws. The FBI is part of the U.S. Department of Justice and has jurisdiction in over 260 types of criminal cases. The FBI maintains an extensive crime laboratory and training facilities, which are regularly made available to other law enforcement agencies. Its vast files—with everything from fingerprint records and criminal aliases to shoe prints and carpet fiber samples—can also be tapped to help with criminal investigations.

SPECIAL AGENT
What You'll Do on the Job

Due to the broad scope of the FBI's law enforcement mission, Special Agents can be put to work on literally hundreds of types of cases. Among these are investigations into organized crime; bank robberies; espionage; terrorism; civil rights violations; embezzlement; extortion; bribery; fraud; public corruption; finance, commerce and trade law violations; kidnapping; and attacks or assassination attempts on federal officials. (Note: Special Agents who enter the FBI ranks with specialized experience or education may be assigned to cases that require their particular expertise. See the information on entrance programs under the "Qualifications" section below.)

While Special Agents usually work on high-security cases and have the FBI's sophisticated resources at their disposal, their basic duties are common to most investigative work. They are seeking facts and evidence that can be used to expose and solve criminal cases. This may involve undercover activities and surveillance operations; reviewing relevant records and documentation; questioning informants, witnesses and suspects; and arresting suspects and seizing evidence.

Special Agents document the methods and results of their investigations in detailed reports. The information and evidence they gather is then submitted to the U.S. Attorney General for any legal action that may be justified. They also assist in preparing cases for trial and testify in court when needed.

Qualifications

To qualify as an FBI Special Agent, you must be a U.S. citizen between the ages of 23 and 37. You will need to take a series of written tests which are computer-scored at FBI headquarters in Washington, D.C. After passing these tests, you will participate in a formal interview. You also must pass a thorough background investigation and physical exam (including vision and hearing tests). Candidates typically need to rank well above average in each area to be considered, due both to the nature of the work and the high level of competition for these positions.

The FBI has established five entrance programs under which Special Agent candidates may qualify. These programs take into account a candidate's education and work experience based on these general guidelines:

1. Law—graduates of an ABA-accredited law school who have 2 years of resident undergraduate work
2. Accounting—graduates of an accredited four-year college or university with a degree in accounting
3. Language—graduates of an accredited four-year college or university who are fluent in a foreign language for which the FBI has a current need
4. Diversified—graduates of an accredited four-year college or university who have at least three years full-time work experience
5. Engineering/Science—graduates of an accredited college or university who have either (a) a master's or other advanced degree in engineering or computer science; or (b) a bachelor's degree in engineering or computer science and at least three years of work experience

Training Involved
Newly appointed Special Agents receive training at the FBI Academy in Quantico, Virginia. Training lasts approximately 16 weeks and consists of classroom instruction in a number of subject areas, a physical fitness program and firearms training.

Applying for the Job
The FBI uses a centralized hiring system that is not subject to OPM appointment regulations. Applications

should be submitted to the nearest FBI field office or to FBI headquarters in Washington, D.C. More information on testing and application procedures is available through an FBI field office or at its headquarters (Federal Bureau of Investigation, Ninth Street & Pennsylvania Avenue, Washington, D.C. 20535).

FEDERAL PROTECTIVE SERVICE

The Federal Protective Service (FPS) is the security branch of the U.S. General Services Administration (GSA), the large government agency that performs numerous management functions related to civilian work sites owned or leased by the federal government. One of the GSA's most important functions—that of ensuring the protection of life and property at these work sites nationwide—is carried out by the Federal Protective Service.

The FPS maintains a mobile, uniformed police force known as Federal Protective Officers. These officers enforce laws, provide security services and perform general policing duties on GSA-controlled federal properties. The FPS also maintains a force of nonuniformed criminal investigators who investigate crimes committed on these properties, often working with local and other law enforcement agencies.

FEDERAL PROTECTIVE OFFICER
What You'll Do on the Job
Establishing proper security measures and preserving law and order are the chief responsibilities of Federal Protective Officers. These officers are assigned to civilian work sites that are owned or leased by the federal government. Their efforts seek to protect employees and visitors to these work sites as well as the actual physical property, buildings and grounds.

Federal Protective Officers must put in place both the personnel and equipment needed to provide adequate and effective security. Officers regularly patrol the facilities and grounds in their charge, checking for signs of intrusion, damage, tampering or unsafe conditions. Guards are typically stationed at entrances to make sure that only federal employees and authorized visitors are admitted. The other aspect of these officers' work involves monitoring diverse electronic security systems. These range from fire alarm equipment to surveillance devices designed to detect intruders, criminal activity or safety hazards.

The law enforcement role of Federal Protective Officers focuses on keeping the peace and preventing or suppressing unlawful conduct. They are authorized to question suspects, issue citations, make arrests and seize evidence relative to crimes committed on the federal property to which they are assigned. These crimes could include anything from burglary, physical assault or arson to disturbing the peace, instigating a riot, or unlawful assembly. Federal Protective Officers also handle emergency situations such as fires, bomb threats and natural disasters. Crowd control services are an important part of their duties, both in times of emergency and during group demonstrations and riots.

Qualifications

To qualify for this position, you must be a U.S. citizen at least 21 years old. In addition, you will need to pass a written test; personal interview; physical examination (including vision and hearing tests); drug screening; and a background investigation. Other requirements include at least one year of police experience or an equivalent amount of college education as determined by the Federal Protective Service.

Training Involved

Trainees participate in an 8-week Police Training Course at the Federal Law Enforcement Training Center in Glynco, Georgia. Specialized training is also provided in crowd and riot control techniques and in performing police functions that have an impact on national security.

Applying for the Job

The written test is administered by the OPM. If you pass this test, you will be put on an eligibility list for Federal Protective Officer positions. More information on testing and application procedures is available through the nearest FPS office or the Federal Protective Service, Room 2306, 18th and F Streets N.W., Washington, D.C. 20405. You may also call 202-501-0887 for information.

U.S. CUSTOMS SERVICE

One of the oldest government agencies, the U.S. Customs Service was established in 1789 by the first Congress of the United States. Its primary mission is to regulate and enforce federal patent, trademark and copyright laws, specifically by monitoring ports of entry into the country. In turn, all law enforcement officials employed by the U.S. Customs Services have duties that in one way or another support this overall mission. This includes efforts to prevent and intercept persons engaged in criminal acts such as illegal smuggling of merchandise and goods; revenue fraud on imported or exported goods; drug and arms trafficking; and cargo thefts.

CUSTOMS SPECIAL AGENT
What You'll Do on the Job

The work of Special Agents resembles that of police detectives, although they operate under a much wider scope of authority and territory. The cases they investigate fall under two related categories: stopping and prosecuting illegal imports and exports, and collecting revenue (tariff duties and taxes) owed to the government on legal imports and exports.

The tasks performed by Special Agents depend on the case being investigated. To collect evidence and information, they may review public and private records. They may question suspects, witnesses or other sources. They may carry out complex surveillance or undercover operations, often working with sophisticated technology and equipment. If their investigative work indicates criminal activity, they then take steps necessary to resolve the case. Special Agents have authority to search ships, aircraft and land vehicles. They can seize smuggled goods or illegal shipments of narcotics, arms and other contraband, as well as detain vehicles or vessels used to transport illegal or suspect goods. They also can arrest persons connected with acts that violate federal laws governed by the U.S. Customs Service.

A wide range of cases are handled by Special Agents—everything from drug trafficking by organized crime syndicates, to tax evasion by international businesses that falsify the value of otherwise legal shipments, to individuals failing to declare purchases made while visiting other countries. Whatever the case, an important part of the Special Agent's job is to keep accurate records of their investigations so that criminal charges can be made and supported. In addition, Special Agents frequently are called upon to help prosecutors prepare cases for trial and to testify in court.

Qualifications

To qualify for a Customs Agent position, you must be a U.S. citizen under 37 years old. You will need to take the Treasury Enforcement Agent (TEA) written examination, which is designed to gauge certain basic skills needed for investigative work, such as good judgment, logic, planning and communication skills. Passing the TEA enables you to be put on an eligibility list. You also must pass a physical examination (including vision and hearing tests), a background investigation and a drug screening. In addition, you must have either (a) a bachelor's degree from an accredited college in any field of study, or (b) at least one year of general work experience and two years of related, specialized experience.

Training Involved

Once accepted as a Special Agent recruit, you will participate in a 14-week enforcement training program at the Federal Law Enforcement Training Center in Glynco, Georgia. The program includes written tests, physical performance tests, and graded practical exercises. Areas covered by this training include the use of firearms, undercover and surveillance techniques, rules of evidence and courtroom procedures, customs laws and regulations, and various methods of investigation and law enforcement.

Applying for the Job

The TEA Examination is administered by the OPM. More information on testing and application procedures is available through the U.S. Customs Service, Office of Human Resources, Enforcement Division, P.O. Box 7108, Washington, D.C. 20044.

CUSTOMS INSPECTOR
What You'll Do on the Job

Customs Inspectors have a "hands-on" job tracking violations in federal customs and commerce laws. They are responsible for inspecting not only the personal baggage of travelers entering or leaving the U.S., but also for inspecting large cargo transported by vehicles on land, air and sea. In all cases, Customs Inspectors are trained to know what to look for and how to handle situations where laws have been violated. They also operate on a mixture of common sense, good observational powers and instincts sharpened by experience.

To regulate commercial shipments, Customs Inspectors are authorized to board and examine aircraft, ships, trains and other methods of transport. They may examine documentation that describes cargo being carried as well as the actual cargo to ensure that no smuggling, fraud or theft takes place. On a ship, for example, they may oversee the unloading of cargo containers; question crew and passengers; and conduct physical searches if any criminal activity is suspected. These efforts are aimed at uncovering the transport of illegal goods—such as narcotics or weaponry—plus goods that have been undervalued, have not been reported or that exceed legal limits as to the amount allowed in or out of the country.

In dealing with both U.S. and international travelers, the work of Customs Inspectors is aimed at making sure duty fees are properly assessed and collected on items brought into the country. They have the authority to inspect baggage and search passengers to reveal whether undeclared goods are being carried or illegal goods are being smuggled. Customs Inspectors can detain and question passengers to determine whether intentional fraud was committed. If so, they can seize items as evidence and report the incident for legal action by the U.S. Customs Service. When the situation warrants, they are empowered to place individuals under arrest for later criminal prosecution.

Qualifications

Along with being a U.S. citizen, you must pass a physical examination, a background investigation and a drug test. You will need to have either a bachelor's degree from an accredited college or at least three years of responsible work experience. A written test—the Customs Inspector Examination—is also administered to appli-

cants for this position. However, by meeting certain educational standards you may be eligible for an Outstanding Scholar Program. Specifically, you must have graduated from college either (a) with a grade point average (GPA) of at least 3.4 on a 4.0 scale; or (b) in the upper 10% academically of your graduating class. If you meet either of these standards, the written test may be waived.

Training Involved

As a Customs Inspector recruit, you will participate in an 11-week enforcement training program at the Federal Law Enforcement Training Center in Glynco, Georgia. This training includes a series of written and physical tests as well as graded practical exercises, for example, on firearms proficiency.

Applying for the Job

The Customs Inspector Examination is administered by the Customs Service. More information on testing and application procedures is available through the U.S. Customs Service, Office of Human Resources, Operations Division, P.O. Box 14156, Washington, D.C. 20044.

Three other law enforcement positions are available through the U.S. Customs Service to serve the overall goals of this agency: Canine Enforcement Officer; Customs Pilot; and Import Specialist. They each have duties that bring them together with Special Agents and Customs Inspectors regularly to investigate customs-related violations. However, their job qualifications differ in some significant ways. These positions are highly specialized and require certain technical expertise or an aptitude in particular areas, as outlined in the following.

Customs Canine Enforcement Officers are responsible for training and handling dogs to uncover the smuggling of illegal narcotics and dangerous drugs, including marijuana, cocaine, heroin and other controlled substances. These uniformed officers are assigned to ports of entry across the U.S. and play a vital role in searching suspect persons and property. Canine Enforcement Officers are often called in to assist with formal investigations, such as those conducted by Customs Special Agents, leading to the apprehension and arrest of smugglers.

To qualify for this position you must be a U.S. citizen; pass a physical examination, background investigation and a drug screening; and have at least three years of responsible work experience or a bachelor's degree from an accredited college. You will not need to take a written test. Related experience—especially any that demonstrates an affinity for dogs—is an obvious plus.

Those selected as recruits will participate in 10 weeks of enforcement and dog handler training at the U.S. Customs Service Canine Enforcement Training Center located in Front Royal, Virginia. This training includes written and physical tests as well as graded practical exercises, including one on firearms proficiency.

Recruitment bulletins are issued by the OPM when the Customs Service has openings for this position. More information on testing and application procedures is available through the U.S. Customs Service, Office of Human Resources, Operations Division, P.O. Box 14060, Washington, D.C. 20044.

Customs Pilots are licensed, experienced pilots who conduct air surveillance to detect customs violations, using a specially equipped fleet of planes and helicopters maintained by the Customs Service. Their flight duties, for example, could involve identifying illegal traffic crossing the U.S. borders between Mexico and Canada, or pursuing smugglers by air along coastal areas. They are also authorized to detain and question suspects, conduct physical searches and make arrests.

This position has strict technical requirements, which include holding a current Federal Aviation Agency (FAA) commercial pilot's license and passing a current FAA Class I physical examination. In addition, you must be a U.S. citizen under 37 years of age and pass a background investigation and drug screening.

Those selected as recruits will participate in a 16-week enforcement training program at the Federal Law Enforcement Training Center in Glynco, Georgia. This training includes written and physical tests as well as graded practical exercises, including one on firearms proficiency.

The U.S. Customs Service will determine your eligibility based on the application you submit and your Record of Aeronautical Experience (Form OPM-1170-21). More information on testing and application procedures is available through the U.S. Customs Service, Office of Human Resources, Delegated Examining Unit/Pilots, P.O. Box 14060, Washington, D.C. 20044.

Customs Import Specialists perform a variety of administrative and investigative functions, primarily related to revenue collection on imported goods. The word "specialist" in their title indicates their skill in appraising the value of commercial imports and calculating payments due to the government on such shipments. Working with other customs officials, Import Specialists may call for and assist in formal investigations into illegally suspect shipments, incidents of fraud and schemes aimed at dodging tariff and trade laws.

Requirements for this position include being a U.S. citizen under 37 years of age and passing a physical examination, background investigation and drug screening. A written test is required, which is explained below. You also must have at least three years of progressively responsible work experience or equivalent education (one year of college equals 9 months of work experience). To help gauge your own interest in this position, keep in mind that enforcing the law in this case means having an aptitude for math, economics, paperwork and understanding complex trade regulations.

Once accepted as a recruit, you will participate in 6 weeks of technical training at the Federal Law Enforcement Training Center in Glynco, Georgia. This training includes a series of written and graded practical exercises.

The written test given for this position—the ACWA (Administrative Careers With America) Examination for Law Enforcement and Investigative Positions—is administered by the OPM. You will need to submit an Admission Notice and Record Card (Form 5000-B) to the OPM location where you want to take the test. The OPM will return the Admission Notice to you to tell you when and where to report for the test. More information on testing and application procedures is available through the U.S. Customs Service, Office of Human Resources, Operations Division, P.O. Box 14156, Washington, D.C. 20044.

U.S. IMMIGRATION AND NATURALIZATION SERVICE

Federal laws regarding the immigration and naturalization of non-U.S. citizens are regulated and enforced by the U.S. Immigration and Naturalization Service (INS). The responsibilities of this agency include apprehending and deporting persons trying to illegally enter the country. It also performs criminal investigations, port-of-entry inspection duties, and background investigations related to persons applying for U.S. citizenship.

BORDER PATROL AGENT
What You'll Do on the Job

Border Patrol Agents are a mobile, uniformed law enforcement corps assigned to guard the borders of the U.S.—roughly 8,000 miles of land and coastal territory. Their chief duty is to detect and prevent the smuggling or entry of illegal aliens into the U.S.

Surveillance and search efforts make up a large part of a Border Patrol Agent's work. To comb the vast and often desolate regions under their watch, they make use of specially equipped pursuit vehicles (cars and jeeps), helicopters, aircraft and patrol boats. State-of-the-art communications systems aid the efforts of teams working together from different modes of transportation. Ground points are set up with sensor equipment that sounds alarms at stationary duty posts when motion is detected. Border Patrol Agents also rely on the basics—good eyesight and standard-issue binoculars—to observe any signs of illegal border activity.

The detective work of this position includes looking for and tracking physical evidence of illegal entry, such as footprints, tire tracks and slashed or broken fences. It involves investigating leads and conducting routine inquiries to uncover smuggling operations, for example, checking the citizenship and immigration status of farm and ranch workers. In addition, Border Patrol Agents set up highway traffic stops and search public transportation sites and vehicles (buses, trucks, trains, airplanes and boats) to identify illegal aliens. Their powers of arrest do not require a warrant. They provide assistance in the criminal prosecution or deportation of illegal aliens they have taken into custody; and in the criminal prosecution of individuals involved in smuggling illegal aliens. They often assist as well in court proceedings regarding petitions for citizenship.

Qualifications

Applicants for Border Patrol Agent positions must be U.S. citizens who are under 37 years of age at the time of appointment. You will need to pass a written civil service examination administered by the OPM, as well as a personal interview, physical examination (including vision and hearing tests) and background investigation. Work experience is required, either paid or voluntary, although a full four-year course of college undergraduate study may be substituted for work experience.

A specific job requirement for active Border Patrol Agents is the ability to read and speak Spanish at a level rated from good to excellent. If you have this ability at the time you apply, you will be given additional credit in the hiring process. Otherwise, you will be expected to develop this ability by the time you complete a one-year probationary period on the job.

Something else to consider before applying is that your first assignment will be in the southwest states bordering Mexico; either California, Arizona, New Mexico or Texas.

Training Involved

Trainees to this position participate in an 18-week training program at the Border Patrol Academy located at the Federal Law Enforcement Training Center in Glynco, Georgia. This training covers areas such as immigration and naturalization laws, criminal law, methods of tracking, pursuit driving, arrest techniques and firearms.

Applying for the Job

To find out when the appropriate civil service examination will be given by the OPM, you can contact a nearby OPM office or write to the Border Patrol's Special Examining Unit which is operated by the INS. More information on testing and application procedures is available through the Immigration and Naturalization Service, Border Patrol Examining Unit, 425 I Street N.W., 2nd floor, Washington, D.C. 20536-0001.

Other law enforcement jobs available through the INS include Special Agent and Immigration Inspector positions. As outlined below, each is responsible for specific aspects of this agency's overall mission of enforcing federal immigration and naturalization laws.

INS Special Agents are nonuniformed officers who plan and conduct investigations aimed at uncovering violations of criminal and statutory laws regulated by the INS. Special Agents gather information and evidence through a review of public and private records and immigration documents, as well as by questioning informants, witnesses and suspects. They may set up complex surveillance and undercover operations. When criminal violations are uncovered, they have authority to arrest suspects and seize evidence. When suspects are brought to trial, Special Agents assist in preparing the prosecution's case and may be called on to testify in court.

Applicants must be U.S. citizens between the ages of 21 and 37 at the time of appointment, although the upper age limitation may be waived if you now hold, or have held in the past, a federal law enforcement position. You will need to pass a personal interview, physical examination (including vision and hearing tests) and background investigation. Either a bachelor's degree, three years of work experience, or an equivalent combination of education and experience are also required.

New recruits participate in an 18-week training program at the Federal Law Enforcement Training Center in Glynco, Georgia, which includes courses in immigration and naturalization laws, investigative techniques and other areas relevant to this position.

To apply, you need to establish an eligible rating with the OPM either by taking a written test or completing a questionnaire describing your previous experience. More information on testing and application procedures is available through the Immigration and Naturalization Service, Personnel Division, 425 I Street N.W., Washington, D.C. 20536 or by calling 202-514-2530.

INS Immigration Inspectors are responsible for preventing the entry of ineligible persons, and admitting eligible persons, into the U.S. These uniformed officials are stationed at land ports, seaports, airports and other places where travelers arrive from other countries. From these locations, Immigration Inspectors process literally millions of people each year, examining passports, visas and other legal documentation required to enter the U.S. An important part of their job is to keep up to date on the laws, regulations, policies, and court and administrative decisions that govern whether persons are eligible for entry.

Requirements for this position include being a U.S. citizen; passing a personal interview, physical examination (including vision and hearing tests) and a background investigation; and having either a bachelor's degree or at least three years of responsible work experience. No minimum or maximum age limits are imposed.

Selected applicants participate in a 14-week training program at the Federal Law Enforcement Training Center in Glynco, Georgia. This includes courses in the Spanish language, nationality laws and firearms proficiency.

For information on testing and application procedures, you may contact either the OPM or the nearest INS regional office in either South Burlington, Vermont; Dallas, Texas; Fort Snelling, Minnesota; or Laguna Niguel, California.

U.S. MARSHALS SERVICE

The U.S. Marshals Service provides security in the federal courts as well as investigative and security services related to federal prisoners and fugitives. This agency also administers the Witness Protection Program formed under the Organized Crime Act of 1970, safeguarding witnesses who testify against organized crime activities in federal and state court cases. The Marshals Service was established in 1789, making it the country's oldest federal law enforcement agency. Deputy U.S. Marshals are hired to carry out the responsibilities of this agency. Their duties are directed by U.S. Marshals, who are appointed by the U.S. President to head the 94 Judicial Districts across the country.

DEPUTY U.S. MARSHAL
What You'll Do on the Job

As officers of the federal court, Deputy U.S. Marshals coordinate security operations during federal court cases. This involves the personal protection of federal judges, attorneys and other court officials and participants. It also involves making sure that proper security systems and personnel are in place throughout federal court buildings. Their role is similar to that of bailiffs during state and local trials—maintaining order in the courtroom, restraining violent actions, conducting weapons searches, serving as guards and escorts. In addition, they serve court orders, such as subpoenas or criminal warrants; seize and dispose of or manage property obtained from criminal activities; and maintain custody of federal prisoners. This includes providing custodial and other services for federal witnesses against organized crime who are protected under the Witness Protection Program.

Another significant area of responsibility has to do with tracking down federal fugitives, for example, those who have escaped from custody, violated parole or probation guidelines, or failed to obey orders to appear in federal court. Such investigations are conducted by Deputy U.S. Marshals in their role as law enforcement agents of the Attorney General, U.S. Department of Justice. They may be required to pursue and arrest a fugitive who has fled to another state or outside U.S. borders. They also assist foreign countries by helping to locate fugitives wanted for prosecution who have escaped to the U.S.

One highly trained unit of the Marshals Service is called the Special Operations Group (SOG). This group of Deputy U.S. Marshals offers fast, specialized assistance during national emergencies in any U.S. Judicial District. They are on call 24 hours a day and can be assembled within hours to intervene in situations such as a large-scale public riot or a crisis triggered by terrorist actions. The SOG is a voluntary unit, but membership is restricted to only the most qualified, skilled and physically fit. Members go through specialized training to determine their eligibility.

Qualifications

To qualify for a Deputy U.S. Marshal position, you must be a U.S. citizen between the ages of 21 and 37 at the time of appointment. You will need to pass a written test, which is administered by the OPM, as well as a personal interview, a physical exam (including vision, hearing and physical performance tests), and a background investigation. Minimum requirements regarding education and experience will be satisfied with either a bachelor's degree from an accredited college or university; three years of responsible work experience; or an equivalent combination of education and experience. (One academic year of full-time undergraduate study is equivalent to nine months of work experience.)

Training Involved

As a Deputy U.S. Marshal trainee, you will need to complete a 13-week basic training program at the Federal Law Enforcement Training Center in Glynco, Georgia. This training consists of an eight-week Criminal Investigator's course and five weeks of courses related to the specific duties of a Deputy U.S. Marshal.

Applying for the Job

You can find out dates that the written test will be given by contacting the OPM or a U.S. Marshals Service field office. More information on testing and application procedures is available through the U.S. Marshals Service, Personnel Management Division, Law Enforcement Recruiting Branch, 600 Army Navy Drive, Arlington, VA 22202-4210. The agency's testing information number is 202-307-9437.

U.S. SECRET SERVICE

When the Secret Service was founded in 1865, its mission was to investigate cases related to the counterfeiting of U.S. currency. That's still a major responsibility of this agency today, along with uncovering other forms of currency fraud. Probably the more well-known responsibility of the Secret Service, however, has to do with protecting the U.S. President, Vice President, their families and other government officials. Special Agents of the Secret Service handle security operations when these officials are traveling. Officers in a special unit—the U.S. Secret Service Uniformed Division—provide security at the White House, at the official residence of the Vice President, and at foreign diplomatic missions primarily in the Washington, D.C. area.

SPECIAL AGENT
What You'll Do on the Job

Special Agents are charged with the duty of protecting:

- the President, Vice President, President-elect and Vice President-elect and their immediate families;
- former Presidents, their spouses or widows (until remarriage), and their minor children;
- major Presidential and Vice Presidential candidates within 120 days of a general Presidential election; and
- visiting heads of foreign states or governments.

Special Agents also may be assigned by the President to guard other foreign dignitaries visiting the U.S. or official representatives of the U.S. while they are on missions abroad.

A significant part of these protective duties is the planning that goes into making sure all necessary security measures are in place for public appearances. An advance team of Special Agents will scope out locations to determine such things as methods of transportation, travel routes, the type of personnel and security equipment needed, and alternate routes and facilities to be used in case of emergency. Special Agents make use of highly sophisticated communications and surveillance equipment to carry out their assignments. They also rely upon other federal, state and local law enforcement agencies for assistance with anything from background information to equipment and personnel.

The other major area of responsibility for Special Agents involves the investigation of currency fraud. This includes counterfeiting operations; the forgery or theft of U.S. Government checks, bonds and securities; and credit card, computer and electronic transfer fraud. Special Agents gather background data and evidence, sometimes calling for surveillance and/or undercover work. They question informants, witnesses and sus-

pects, and have authority to arrest suspects and seize evidence. When cases are brought to trial, Special Agents assist U.S. Attorneys through their verbal and written reports and by giving testimony in court.

Qualifications

Requirements for the position of Special Agent include being a U.S. citizen under age 37 at the time of appointment to duty. You must pass a written test (the Treasury Enforcement Agent Examination), a personal interview, a polygraph test, background investigation and medical exam (including vision and hearing tests) conducted by the Secret Service. A bachelor's degree from an accredited college or university in any field of study is also required. You may be able to qualify instead with at least three years work experience, two of those in criminal investigative work; or with the equivalent in relevant work experience and education. In addition, because of the nature of this job, you must be willing to travel and relocate at any time.

Training Involved

Once accepted as a Special Agent recruit, you'll receive general investigative training at the Federal Law Enforcement Training Center in Glynco, Georgia; and specialized instruction at Secret Service training facilities near Washington, D.C. This training includes courses in protective techniques, criminal law, the use of firearms, defensive measures, surveillance techniques and undercover operations.

Applying for the Job

To apply and sign up to take the Treasury Enforcement Agent (TEA) Examination, you may contact the nearest OPM office or Secret Service field office. More information on testing and application procedures is available through the U.S. Secret Service Personnel

In addition to those described above, Special Agent and Criminal Investigator positions are also available through the following federal agencies:

Department of Defense
Office of Inspector General
Personnel Division
400 Army Navy Drive
Arlington, VA 22202-2884
Position: Special Agent—Defense Criminal Investigative Service

Internal Revenue Service
1111 Constitution Avenue N.W., Room 1034
Washington, D.C. 20224
Position: Special Agent

U.S. Air Force
Office of Special Investigations
Bolling Air Force Base
Washington, D.C. 20332-6001
Position: Criminal Investigator

S. Department of Labor
ice of Inspector General
an Resources Management Division
Constitution Avenue N.W., Room S-5513
ngton, D.C. 20210
: *Criminal Investigator*

al Investigative Service
vices Department
, D.C. 20388-5025
ial Agent

FEDERAL POLICE OFFICERS

The National Park Service Park Police is a force maintained by the National Park Service (NPS), a division of the U.S. Department of the Interior that is responsible for conserving and managing designated recreational, cultural, historical and natural areas nationwide. *Park Police Officers* are under the employment of the National Capitol Region in Washington, D.C. They provide law enforcement services within this metropolitan area, where the largest group of officers are assigned, as well as in other NPS areas. Along with ongoing standard policing duties, these officers perform specific functions such as: crowd control during large public gatherings and civic events conducted on NPS lands, protection services for federal government officials and visiting foreign heads of state, and emergency assistance for other NPS areas and other federal agencies. This police force includes horse-mounted, motorcycle, vehicular, helicopter and canine units. Other major areas of employment are the Gateway National Recreation Area in New York City and the Golden Gate National Recreation Area in San Francisco.

To qualify for this position, you must be a U.S. citizen between 21 and 31 years of age. You will need to pass a written test, oral interview, physical examination (including vision, hearing and physical performance tests), and background investigation. Other requirements include either two years of study at an accredited college or university or two years of work experience.

Trainees participate in an 18-week training program at the Federal Law Enforcement Training Center in Glynco, Georgia. This is followed by additional on-the-job training under the supervision of an experienced field training officer.

The written test for this position is a civil service exam administered by the OPM. Military personnel may

---

Division, 1800 G Street, N.W., Washington, D.C. 20223, or by calling 1-800-827-7783.

UNIFORMED DIVISION OFFICER
What You'll Do on the Job

Performing high-level security and law enforcement functions are the chief duties of the Secret Service Uniformed Division. Officers in this division are assigned to the Washington, D.C. metropolitan area to cover security for:

- the White House grounds and any buildings which house presidential offices
- the official residence of the Vice President
- foreign diplomatic missions or embassies located in the District of Columbia (or other regions under special order of the President)

The Uniformed Division functions much like a police force, constantly on the watch for any disturbances, suspicious situations and criminal activity. Officers ensure that all necessary security systems and equipment are in place. They conduct regular patrols to monitor the grounds, buildings and security equipment in their assigned areas. Fixed security posts are used at entrance/exit points to ensure that visitors are authorized to be on the premises. Officers have the authority to question, search and arrest trespassers or others involved in illegal or disruptive activities. Officers assigned to canine teams may be called in to investigate incidents such as bomb threats.

Qualifications

To qualify for the Uniformed Division, you must be a U.S. citizen under age 37 at the time of appointment. Once you have passed a written exam, you will go through a personal interview. You must also pass a background investigation, polygraph test, and medical examination (including vision and hearing tests). A high school diploma or GED satisfies the minimum educational requirements.

Training Involved

Uniformed Division Officer recruits are trained at the Federal Law Enforcement Training Center in Glynco, Georgia, and receive specialized instruction at Secret Service training facilities near Washington D.C. This training includes courses in police procedures; psychology; police-community relations; criminal law; first aid; laws of arrest, search and seizure; use of firearms; and physical defense techniques.

Applying for the Job

Tests and interviews are conducted by the Secret Service. The written examination is usually given on a quarterly basis in the Washington, D.C. area and periodically in other major U.S. cities. To apply to take the test, you need to submit a 3x5 index card or postcard stating your name, address and telephone numbers (home and work). On this card, also indicate where you want to be tested—in Washington, D.C., in a major city in your area, or in any city where the test is given. Send this card to: U.S. Secret Service, Attn: Uniformed Division Recruiter, 1800 G Street, N.W., Washington, D.C. 20223. More information on testing and application procedures is available through the address given above or by calling 1-800-827-7783.

OTHER FEDERAL AGENCY POSITIONS

This section highlights federal law enforcement positions that fall under two main job categories: (1) special agents and criminal investigators; and (2) police officers. In addition to some of these described in more detail above, a sampling of job descriptions in these categories is provided here, along with lists of several other federal agencies that offer these positions.

FEDERAL SPECIAL AGENTS AND CRIMINAL INVESTIGATORS

The U.S. Department of State provides services related to overseas diplomatic, commercial and cultural affairs, including the administration of U.S. foreign policy. *Special Agents* for the Department of State carry out various security duties, such as protecting foreign dignitaries and Department of State officials and serving as Security Officers to protect overseas embassies or consulates. Investigative activities are another aspect of their work. For example, Special Agents have primary jurisdiction in conducting criminal investigations involving passport and visa fraud. They also handle background investigations on Department of State employees.

To qualify for this position, you must be a U.S. citizen between the ages of 21 and 35. You will need to pass a written essay test; personal interview; physical examination (including vision, hearing and physical performance tests); drug screening exam; and background investigation. A bachelor's degree is required, along with at least one year of work experience or the equivalent in education beyond the bachelor's degree.

Trainees participate in an 8-week general training program at the Federal Law Enforcement Training Center in Glynco, Georgia. This is followed by 9 to 12 weeks of training in duties specific to this position, which takes place in the Washington, D.C. area. Further training is required for Special Agents who are assigned to overseas duty stations.

Applications, which may need to include a resume or Optional Application for Federal Employment, a brief personal biography and a copy of your college transcripts, should be sent directly to the Department of State. You will be scheduled for the written test and

oral interview at a time when the Department of State is hiring. If you earn passing scores, you will be placed on an eligibility list for up to 18 months. More information on testing and application procedures is available through the U.S. Department of State, Recruitment Division, P.O. Box 9317, Arlington, VA 22219. You may also call the agency's Foreign Service Career Line at 703-875-7490.

The Bureau of Land Management (BLM) is a division of the U.S. Department of the Interior whose primary responsibility is the management of federally owned public lands that consist of forests and ranges. The chief area of responsibility for *Criminal Investigators* employed by this agency involves conducting investigations into crimes committed on properties under the jurisdiction of the BLM. Such crimes could range from the theft of archaeological artifacts to the destruction or illegal removal of timber.

To qualify for this position, you must be a U.S. citizen between the ages of 21 and 37 at the time of appointment. No written test is required, but you must pass a personal interview, physical examination (including vision and hearing tests) and background investigation. You also need to hold either a four-year degree from an accredited college or university or the equivalent in work experience.

Trainees participate in an 8-week Criminal Investigators training program at the Federal Law Enforcement Training Center in Glynco, Georgia. (If you already have experience in criminal investigative work, you may be eligible to attend a condensed 5-week training program.)

To apply, you will need to submit a resume, an Optional Application for Federal Employment or some other written application to the BLM. These positions are filled based on prior experience and training. More information on testing and application procedures is

available through the U.S. Department of the Interior, Bureau of Land Management, Personnel Service, 18th & C Streets N.W., Washington, D.C. 20240.

The Bureau of Indian Affairs (BIA) is a division of the U.S. Department of the Interior whose jurisdiction includes reservations and lands that are owned by Indians (Native Americans) and governed by their Tribal laws. *Criminal Investigators* for the BIA are responsible for investigating, making arrests and assisting in the prosecution of federal crimes that are committed on Indian lands within the BIA's jurisdiction. Other federal, state and local law agencies often enlist the services of BIA Criminal Investigators to locate criminal suspects alleged or known to be living on Native American lands.

To qualify for this position, you must be a U.S. citizen between the ages of 21 and 35. You will need to pass a personal interview, physical examination (including vision and hearing tests) and a background investigation. You also need to have completed four years of study at an accredited college or university or have the equivalent in experience. Typically, no written test is required, although one may be administered by the OPM periodically to establish an eligibility list for the BIA.

Trainees for this position participate in an 8-week Criminal Investigator Course at the Federal Law Enforcement Training Center in Glynco, Georgia.

Qualified Native American applicants are given priority in the hiring process for Criminal Investigator positions; those eligible under the Indian Preference Act can apply directly to the BIA for any current openings. More information on testing and application procedures is available through the Bureau of Indian Affairs, Personnel Service, 1951 Constitution Avenue N.W., Washington, D.C. 20245. You may also call the job hotline at 202-208-2682.

The Fish and Wildlife Service (FWS) is an agency of the U.S. Department of the Interior authorized to manage, protect and conserve the country's fish and wildlife resources. *Special Agents* of the FWS conduct investigations involving the criminal violation of federal fish and wildlife laws. Their duties are common to most investigative work, such as setting up surveillance operations, questioning informants and suspects, collecting evidence and arresting suspects. However, their investigations are rather unique in nature due to their focus on enforcing federal laws that safeguard birds, mammals, reptiles, mollusks, crustacea and other wildlife and fish.

To qualify for this position, you must be a U.S. citizen between the ages of 21 and 37. You will need to pass a written test, personal interview, physical examination (including vision and hearing tests) and background investigation. You also need to have either a four-year degree in any field of study from an accredited or university; at least three years of work ex or the equivalent combination of edu experience.

Trainees participate in a 14-week covering various law enforcement niques at the Federal Law Enforce ter in Glynco, Georgia. This is training at one of seven design tricts in the U.S.

The OPM adminis erates an eligibility list Test dates are annou tact the FWS direc jected job open application p and Wildli 18th and may a hot

apply to the OPM to take the examination within 120 days prior to, or within 120 days after, honorable discharge. More information on testing and application procedures is available through the U.S. Park Police, Personnel Office, 1100 Ohio Drive S.W., Washington, D.C. 20242. You may also call their job hotline at 202-619-7479 or their personnel office at 202-619-7056.

The U.S. Capitol Police provides law enforcement and investigative services for government officials and offices in Washington, D.C. Specifically, this force of *Capitol Police Officers* serves members of Congress and the Congressional community within the Capitol, House of Representatives and Senate buildings and surrounding streets and parks. The Capitol Police maintains many specialized police units. For example, the Containment and Emergency Response Team unit is trained to counter an armed assault upon the Congress. The Threat Assessment Unit investigates threats made against members of Congress. The Protective Operations Section offers round-the-clock protection to Congressional members anywhere in the country. Among other such specialized units are the K-9 Explosive Detective Section, Patrol Division, Criminal Investigation Division and Electronic Countermeasures Section.

To qualify for this position, you must be a U.S. citizen between 21 and 35 years of age. You will need to pass a written test, personal interview, physical examination (including vision and hearing tests), psychological test, polygraph test, and background investigation. A high school diploma or GED satisfies the educational requirements.

Trainees first participate in a 2-week orientation program at the Capitol Police training facility in Washington, D.C. This is followed by an 8-week Police Training Course at the Federal Law Enforcement Training Center in Glynco, Georgia. An additional 8 weeks of

comprehensive training is then provided back at the Capitol Police training facility.

The written test for this position is administered by the Capitol Police at its headquarters in Washington, D.C. Once you pass this test, you will be given an application and information necessary for further processing. More information on testing (including next test dates) and application procedures is available through the U.S. Capitol Police, Public Information Office, 119 D Street N.E., Washington, D.C. 20510. You may also call 202-224-9819.

The Library of Congress Police handles law enforcement and security services for the Library of Congress, the national library of the U.S. which features vast research materials and historical collections. *Library of Congress Police Officers* are charged with protecting these valuable resources as well as library personnel and visitors. They conduct regular patrols of the library buildings and grounds, inspecting the facilities to detect any safety hazards or property damage. Monitoring security devices is another part of their duties, including electronic or computerized surveillance, fire alarm and entrance-access systems. These officers are also on the lookout for suspicious behavior or criminal activity to prevent public disturbances, acts of violence and other unlawful or unsafe situations.

To qualify for this position, you must be a U.S. citizen with at least one and one-half years of work experience in any type of protective service. This could include experience gained as an armed guard, private detective, police officer or in another job where you were able to develop a general knowledge of law enforcement methods and techniques. However, if you have taken courses above the high school level in police administration or criminology, this education may be substituted for the required work experience. No written test is required. You will need to pass a personal interview, physical examination (including vision and hearing tests), and background investigation.

Trainees participate in an 8-week Police Training Course at the Federal Law Enforcement Training Center in Glynco, Georgia.

To apply, you need to submit a resume, an Optional Application for Federal Employment, or some other written application to the Library of Congress Employment Office. More information on testing and application procedures is available through the Library of Congress Employment Office, James Madison Memorial Building, 101 Independence Avenue S.E., Washington, D.C. 20540. You may also call 202-707-5627.

In addition to those described above, Police Officer positions are also available through the following federal agencies:

U.S. Government Printing Office
Employment Branch, Room C-106, Stop: PWE
North Capitol and H Streets N.W.
Washington, D.C. 20401
Position: Police Officer

U.S. Supreme Court
Personnel Office, Room 3
One First Street N.E.
Washington, D.C. 20543
Position: Police Officer

Department of Defense
Washington Headquarters Services
Personnel and Security
Washington, D.C. 20301-1155
Position: Police Officer—Security of Defense

ON TRAINS, ON CAMPUS, AND IN THE PRIVATE SECTOR

Below you'll find descriptions of other jobs available in policing and in the fast-growing area of private security.

AMTRAK POLICE

If you've ever been aboard an Amtrak train, you may have noticed police officers patrolling the cars. The Amtrak rail service employs approximately 330 police officers nationwide. Because Amtrak typically hires only 20 officers a year, and receives roughly 60-100 resumes for each job opening, these positions are extremely competitive.

The law enforcement responsibilities of these officers are much like those of municipal police officers. They're there to protect Amtrak personnel, passengers and property; to keep the peace; and to maintain law and order. Among the qualifications for joining the Amtrak police, you need to be at least 21 years old and have a clean criminal record and valid driver's license. The minimum educational requirement is either an associate's degree or 60 hours credit from a university or community college. No previous work experience in law enforcement is required. Training includes coursework at your local state police academy and an 8-week basic training session at the Federal Law Enforcement Training Center in Glynco, Georgia.

To apply for an Amtrak police position, send a resume and a cover letter indicating your interest to: Amtrak Personnel, 30th Street Station, 2nd Floor, Philadelphia, PA 19104. You will receive a letter from Amtrak acknowledging that your resume has been received. If you meet the minimum qualifications, your resume will be forwarded to an Amtrak office in your area. You are responsible for contacting that office periodically to check on the hiring status in your area.

(A phone number for your local office will be included in your letter of acknowledgment.)

CAMPUS POLICE

Colleges and universities nationwide are a source of many policing and security jobs. Campus police protect college or university personnel, students and visitors. Mostly on foot and in cars, they patrol the campus grounds and buildings, including administrative offices, classrooms, libraries and dormitories. In addition to patrol duty, university police provide security at university-sponsored events, enforce traffic and parking laws, and settle disturbances on campus, often working in conjunction with the local municipal police.

Depending on the state and school, a campus security force may consist of either sworn or unsworn officers. Sworn officers carry handguns and follow the firearms regulations and training required by state law. Unsworn officers are like private security guards and may carry weapons other than handguns.

Many colleges and universities are members of an organization known as the International Association of Campus Law Enforcement Administrators (IACLEA), which recommends over 200 hiring standards for campus police officers. Even among members of IACLEA, however, the employment requirements, application procedures and training standards for campus police and security positions still vary by institution. Your best bet is to check with the personnel office at the college or university where you wish to work.

PRIVATE SECURITY OFFICERS

Many private businesses and organizations today hire people to perform jobs that are like traditional law enforcement positions—up to a point. Technically speaking, people in these jobs are not authorized to "enforce the law." But they can carry out certain policing, surveillance and security functions; and they can apprehend and turn over individuals involved in criminal acts to the proper legal authorities.

One of the most prominent positions of this nature is that of security officer. According to the U.S. Bureau of Labor Statistics (BLS), security officers held over 800,000 jobs in 1992. More than half of these were employed by industrial security firms and guard agencies, which contract with clients to provide security services and then assign security personnel to client sites. Other major employers include private organizations such as banks, hotels, hospitals, office buildings and retail stores.

Where you are hired as a security officer would determine the exact duties of your job. You may work alone on a shift or as part of a security team. You may or may not carry a gun or other weapon. You could be protecting merchandise, property or equipment from theft or damage. You might be required to patrol an assigned area, outdoors or indoors, checking for possible intruders or safety hazards. You could be assigned to a front desk to sign in/out or examine the credentials of persons wanting access. You may be monitoring computerized or electronic security systems such as surveillance, fire alarm or motion detector devices. You might be in charge of crowd control or more generally keeping the peace to prevent or suppress any disruptive, violent or criminal behavior. Again, which of these responsibilities you hold would depend on the employer.

Here's a list to give you just an idea of the many potential employers of security personnel:

- Retail businesses (department stores, electronic stores, jewelry stores, etc.)
- Shopping malls
- Apartment buildings
- Hotels
- Office buildings

- Banks and other financial institutions
- Computer companies and data processing centers
- Drug manufacturers
- Equipment manufacturers
- Hospitals
- Airports
- Railroad stations
- Factories
- Laboratories
- Recreational parks and facilities
- Resorts and golf courses
- Convention centers
- Sports arenas
- Museums, art galleries and historical buildings
- Libraries

No single set of job requirements exists for security officers in the private sector. For entry-level security personnel, a high school diploma or GED may satisfy educational standards. For non-high school graduates, some employers may offer reading and writing tests to determine an applicant's ability to follow written and oral instructions. Employers may prefer applicants with some related experience, for example, in the military or in police or sheriff's departments, or other experience that demonstrates responsible work habits.

Having good character references and no criminal record can be critical factors. It's also important to be in good health and have good vision and hearing. Employers also look for candidates who are alert, emotionally stable and have good communication skills, especially when hiring for positions that have a great deal of contact with the public. Along with checking character references, employers may run a more formal background check and may require a polygraph test and drug screening.

How much and what kind of training you'll receive also depends on the job and the employer. On-the-job supervised training is standard practice, but many employers first provide formal instruction covering areas such as security techniques, crowd control and first aid. Security personnel who will be carrying a firearm or using sophisticated electronic security systems can expect to undergo formal training and periodic skills testing.

If you're interested in exploring security officer and other security positions, there are several ways to go about it. Contact the personnel offices at various businesses and private organizations and ask about their hiring practices. Check the yellow pages for private security companies in your area. Study the classified ads in the newspapers. Also go straight to the source and talk to a few security officers directly. You can find out how they got hired, what kind of background or experience they had coming in to the position, and how they like the job.

One final note. The BLS reports that most states and the District of Columbia have licensing and registration requirements for security officers who are employed by contract security or guard agencies. To become licensed as a security officer for such agencies, typically you must be at least 18 years old; pass a background investigation; have no criminal convictions for perjury or acts of violence; and complete formal training in subjects such as property rights, emergency procedures, and the seizure of suspected criminals. Some states and the District of Columbia also have licensing and registration requirements for security officers hired privately rather than through agencies. This is the present trend given that more and more private organizations are taking on their own security personnel.

FEDERAL JOB INFORMATION

The following is a list of addresses (alphabetized by state) of Federal Job Information Computer Centers located throughout the United States. These centers are equipped with computer-based systems that use a simple "touch screen" technology. You can tap into on-line information about Federal job opportunities worldwide and request application packages for any jobs that interest you. These sites generally are open to the public Monday through Friday during normal business hours.

After this list are descriptions of other information sources you can access by phone or by using a personal computer and a modem. Last but not least, you can take the more traditional route of visiting your local State Employment Service office. These offices have lists of current job vacancies and open examination schedules, available either on printed reports, microfiche, or via computer.

Job Information Computer Center
520 Wynn Drive NW
Huntsville, AL

Federal Building
222 West Seventh Avenue, Room156
Anchorage, AK

VA Medical Center
650 East Indian School Road
Building 21, Room 147
Phoenix, AZ

Federal Building
700 West Capitol, First Floor Lobby
Little Rock, AR

Job Information Computer Center
9650 Flair Drive, Suite 100A, El Monte
Los Angeles, CA

Federal Building
Room 4260, 880 Front Street
San Diego, CA

Job Information Computer Center
1029 Howard Street, Suite B
San Francisco, CA

Job Information Computer Center
12345 West Alameda Parkway, Lakewood
Denver, CO

Federal Building
450 Main Street, Room 133
Hartford, CT

Theodore Roosevelt Federal Building
1900 E Street NW, Room 1416
Washington, DC

Downtown Jobs and Benefits Center,
Job Service of Florida
401 NW Second Avenue, Suite N-214
Miami, FL

Job Service of Florida
3421 Lawton Road, Suite 100
Orlando, FL

Richard B. Russell Federal Building
Main Lobby, Plaza Level
75 Spring Street SW
Atlanta, GA

Federal Building, Room 5316
300 Ala Moana Boulevard
Honolulu, HI

Department of Army
Army Civilian Personnel Office
Army Garrison, Building T-1500
Fort Shafter, HI

Job Information Computer Center
230 South Dearborn Street, Room 2916
Chicago, IL

Minton-Capehart Federal Building
575 North Pennsylvania Street, Room 368
Indianapolis, IN

Federal Building
423 Canal Street, First Floor Lobby
New Orleans, LA

Federal Office Building
40 Western Avenue
Augusta, ME

George H. Fallon Building
Lombard Street and Hopkins Plaza, Lobby
Baltimore, MD

Thomas P. O'Neill, Jr. Federal Building
10 Causeway Street, Second Floor
Boston, MA

Job Information Computer Center
477 Michigan Avenue, Room 565
Detroit, MI

Bishop Henry Whipple Federal Building
One Federal Drive, Room 501
Fort Snelling, Minnesota

Federal Building
601 East 12th Street, Room 134
Kansas City, MO

Thomas McIntyre Federal Building
80 Daniel Street, First Floor Lobby
Portsmouth, NH

Peter J. Rodino Federal Building
970 Broad Street, Second Floor
Newark, NJ

Job Information Computer Center
505 Marquette Avenue, Suite 910
Albuquerque, NM

Leo W. O'Brian Federal Building
Clinton Avenue and North Pearl, Basement Level
Albany, NY

Thaddeus T. Dulski Federal Building
111 West Huron Street, Ninth Floor
Buffalo, NY

Jacob K. Javits Federal Building
26 Federal Plaza, Lobby
New York, NY

Job Information Computer Center
290 Broadway, Lobby
New York, NY

James M. Hanley Federal Building
100 South Clinton Street
Syracuse, NY

Job Information Computer Center
4407 Bland Road, Suite 202
Raleigh, NC

Federal Building
200 West Second Street, Room 506
Dayton, OH

Career Connection Center
7401 NE 23rd Street
Oklahoma City, OK

Federal Building
1220 SW Third Avenue, Room 376
Portland, OR

Federal Building
228 Walnut Street, Room 168
Harrisburg, PA

William J. Green, Jr. Federal Building
600 Arch Street
Philadelphia, PA

Federal Building
1000 Liberty Avenue, First Floor Lobby
Pittsburgh, PA

Reading Postal Service
2100 North 13th Street
Reading, PA

US Federal Building
150 Carlos Chardon Avenue, Room 328
San Juan, PR

Job Information Computer Center
380 Westminster, Mall Lobby
Providence, RI

Naval Air Station Memphis
Transition Assistance Center
7800 Third Avenue, Building South 239
Millington, TN

Federal Building
1100 Commerce Street, First Floor Lobby
Dallas, TX

Federal Building
700 East San Antonio Street, Lobby
El Paso, TX

Mickey Leland Federal Building
1919 Smith Street, First Floor Lobby
Houston, TX

Job Information Computer Center
8610 Broadway, Room 305
San Antonio, TX

Texas Employment Commission Office
4310 Naco-Perrin
San Antonio, TX

Federal Building
11 Elmwood Avenue, First Floor Lobby
Burlington, VT

Peninsula Civilian Personnel Support Activity
11824 Fishing Point Drive, Suite C
Newport News, VA

Federal Building
200 Granby Street, Second Floor
Norfolk, VA

Federal Building
915 Second Avenue, Room 110
Seattle, WA

Career America Connection

All you need is a telephone to reach the Career America Connection, another resource for federal job information. At the numbers listed below, you can find out about current job vacancies, salaries, benefits and how to apply. Information is also provided about special programs, such as the Presidential Management Intern Program and programs for veterans, students, people with disabilities and other groups. This system is in operation seven days a week, 24 hours a day.

Huntsville, AL
205-837-0894

San Francisco, CA
415-744-5627

Denver, CO
303-969-7050

Washington, DC
202-606-2700

Atlanta, GA
404-331-4315

Honolulu, HI
808-541-2791

Chicago, IL
312-353-6192

Detroit, MI
313-226-6950

Twin Cities, MN
612-725-3430

Raleigh, NC
919-790-2822

Dayton, OH
513-225-2720

Philadelphia, PA
215-597-7440

San Antonio, TX
210-805-2402

Norfolk, VA
804-441-3365

Seattle, WA
206-553-0888

or from anywhere in the world
912-757-3000

Nationwide TDD Service
912-744-2299

On-Line Job Board

If you've got a personal computer, telecommunications software and a modem, check out the Federal Job Opportunities Board (FJOB) by dialing 912-757-3100. Through this on-line system, you can get information about current job listings and federal employment procedures and request applications. If you're familiar with Internet applications, you also can access the FJOB through Telnet and File Transfer Protocol (FTP) at [FJOB.MAIL.OPM.GOV] or at this IP address: [198.78.46.10].

INDEX

Tell Us What You Think!

We hope that the information in this book gives you the edge you need in your job search. To help us do our job even better, we would appreciate your taking a few minutes to answer the brief questions below. PLEASE PRINT OR TYPE YOUR RESPONSES. Thank you for your time — and good luck in your career search!

The title of this book is _____

The most helpful part of this book is _____

This book would be even more helpful if it included information on _____

Other jobs or careers of interest to me are

1. _____   3. _____

2. _____   4. _____

How did you find out about this book?

❑ Ad (appearing in _____)   ❑ Recommended to me

❑ Guidance counselor/career counselor   ❑ Other (please explain) _____

I am currently

❑ A student (level: _____)   ❑ Employed (job title: _____)

❑ Other (please explain) _____

Your Name _____

Street Address _____

City _____ State _____ Zip Code _____

Phone Number _____

Your Age _____

Name of a friend who would be interested in LearningExpress products

Name _____

Street Address _____

City _____ State _____ Zip Code _____

(FOLD HERE AND TAPE OR STAPLE)

LearningExpress
900 BROADWAY
SUITE 604
NEW YORK NY 10003

(FOLD HERE AND TAPE OR STAPLE)

4